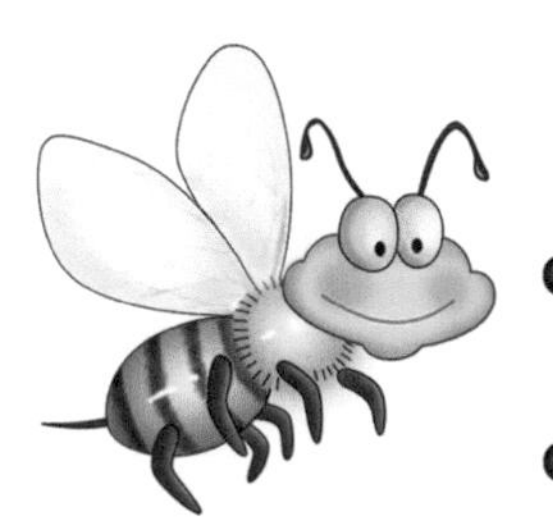

I CAN WRITE abc

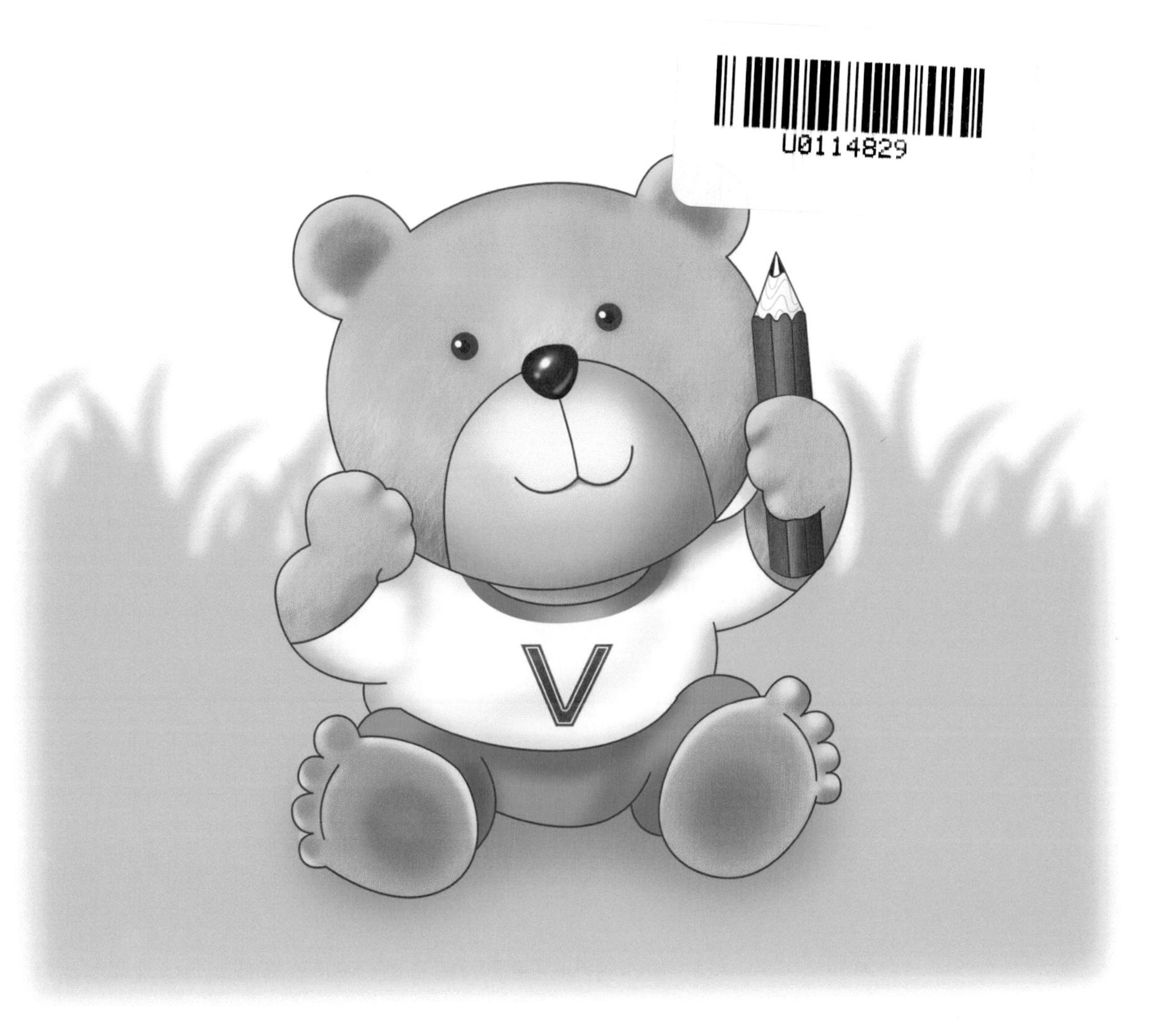

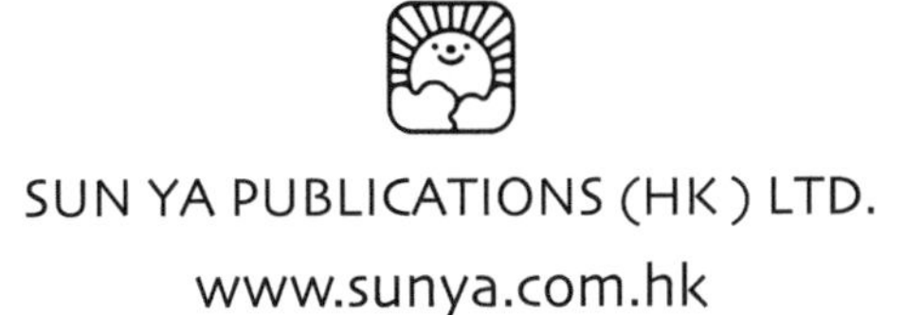

SUN YA PUBLICATIONS (HK) LTD.
www.sunya.com.hk

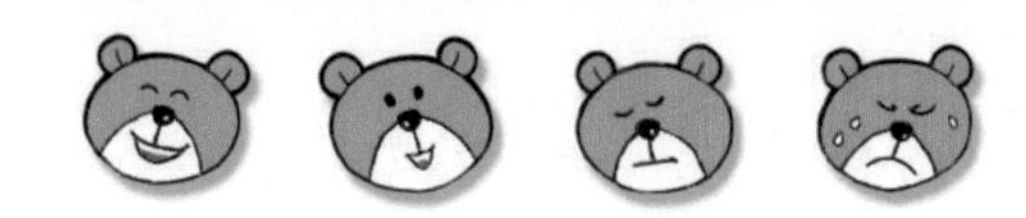

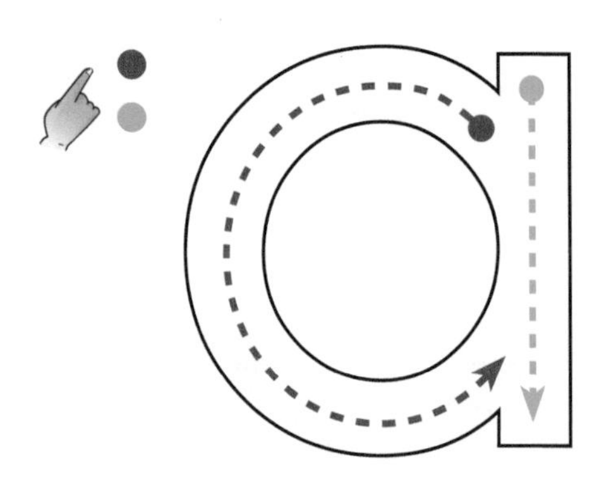

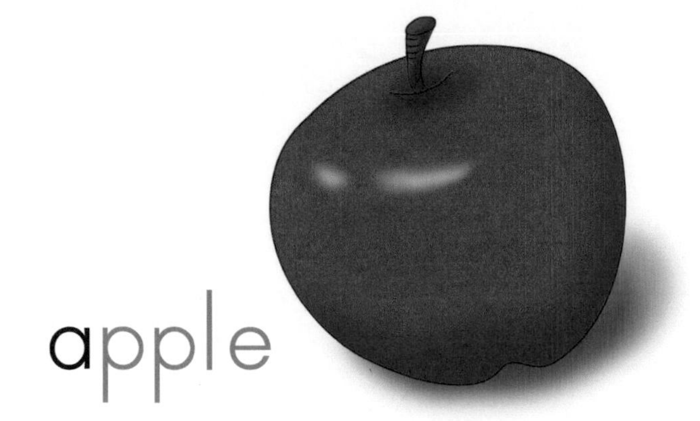

畫一畫
Trace the Lines

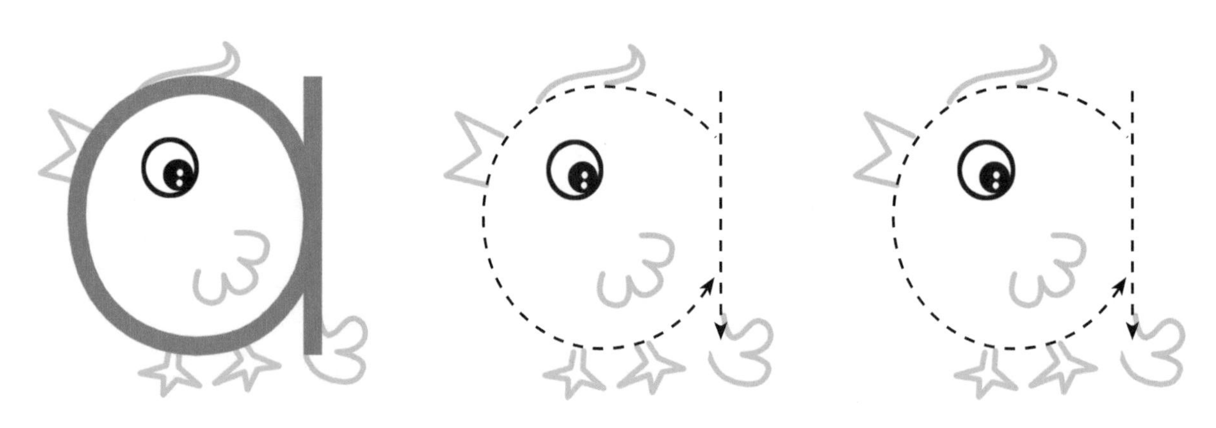

寫一寫
Trace and write

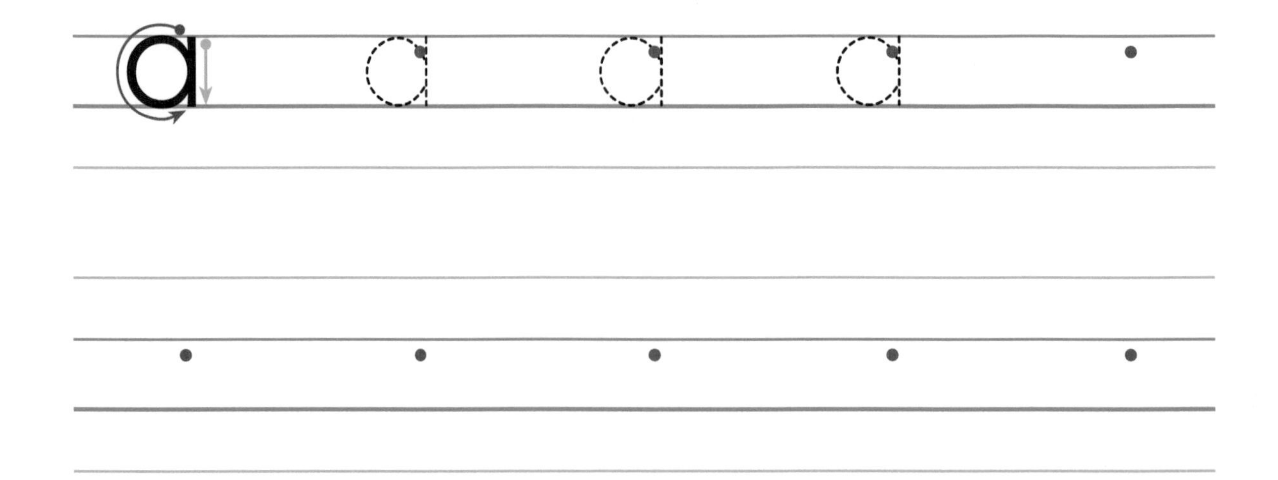

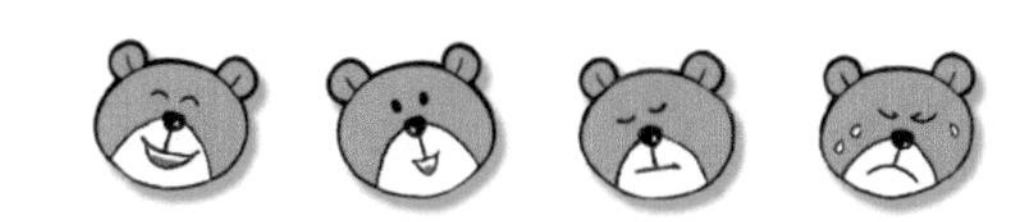

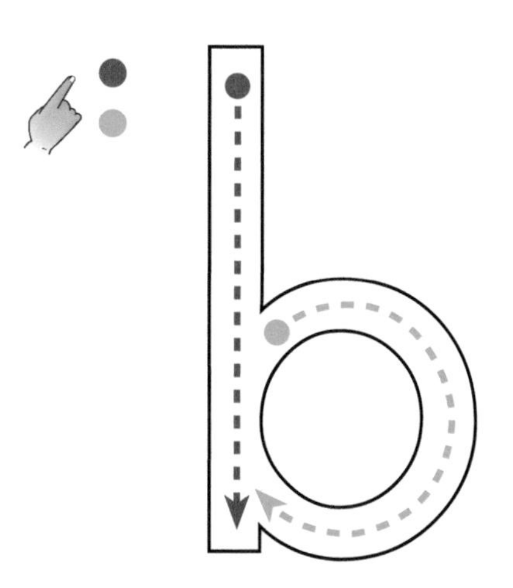

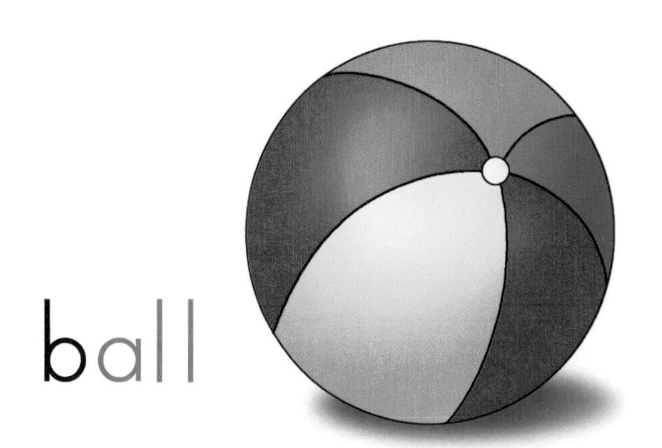

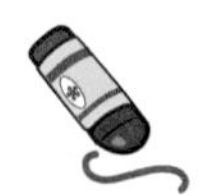

畫一畫
Trace the Lines

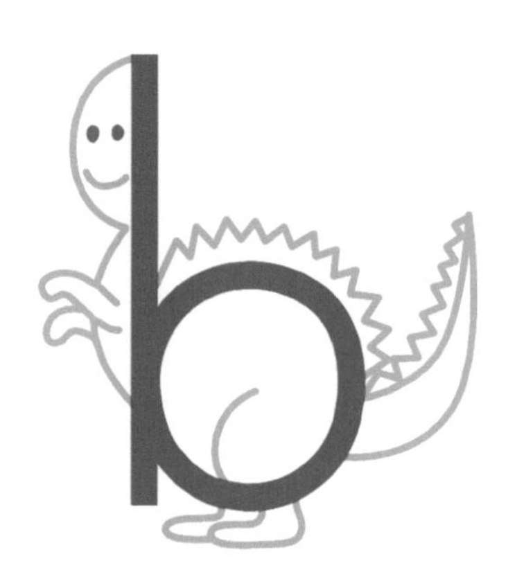

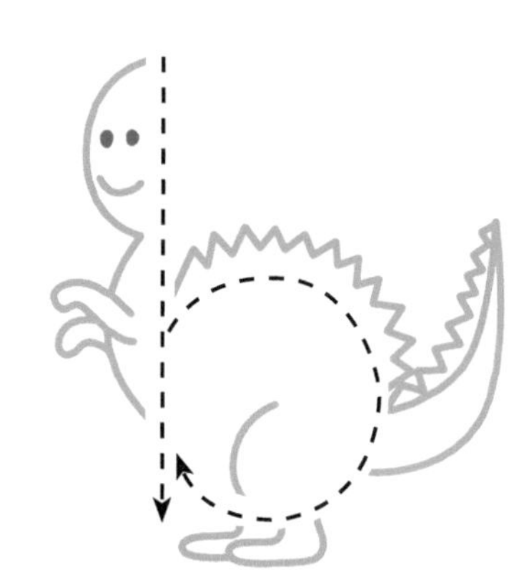

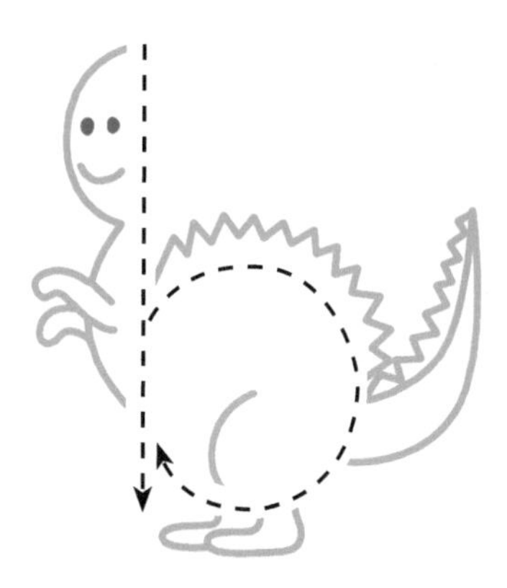

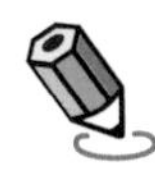

寫一寫
Trace and write

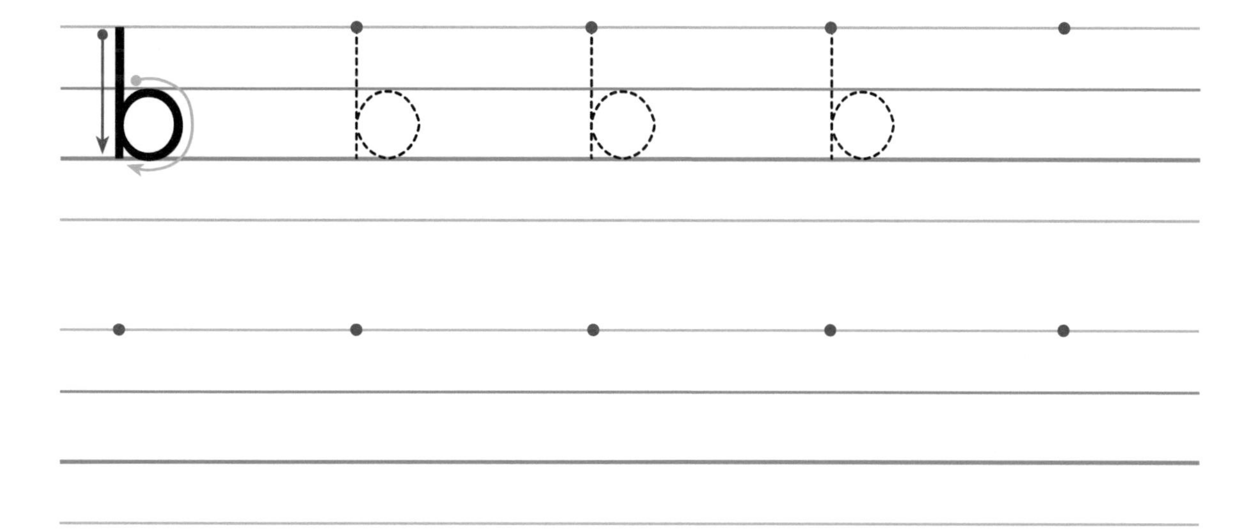

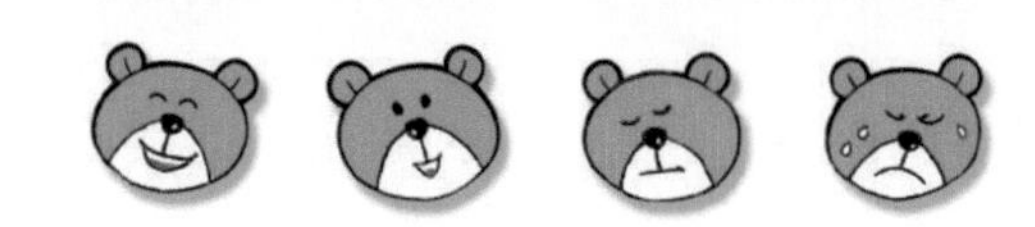

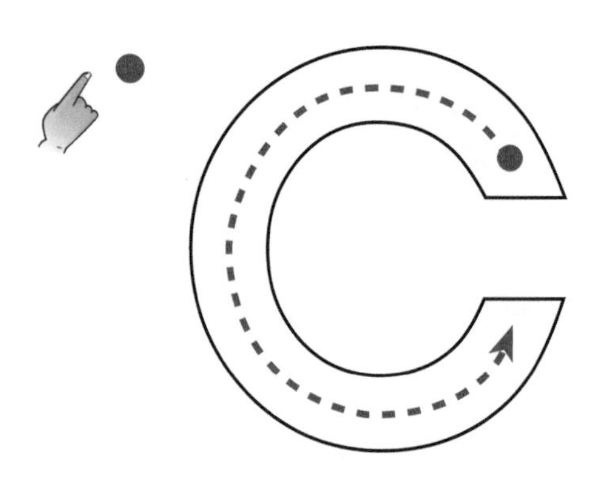

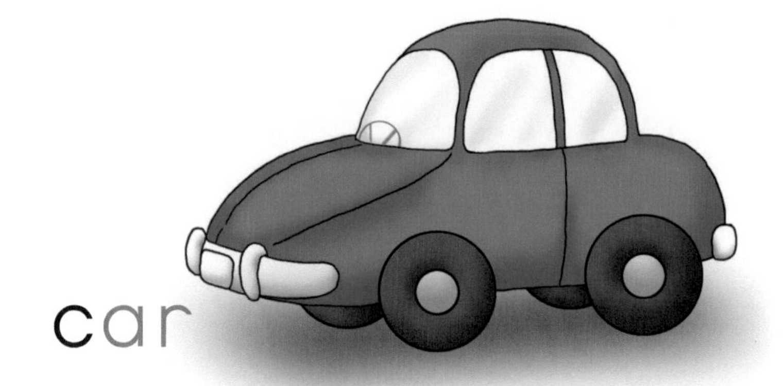

car

畫一畫

Trace the Lines

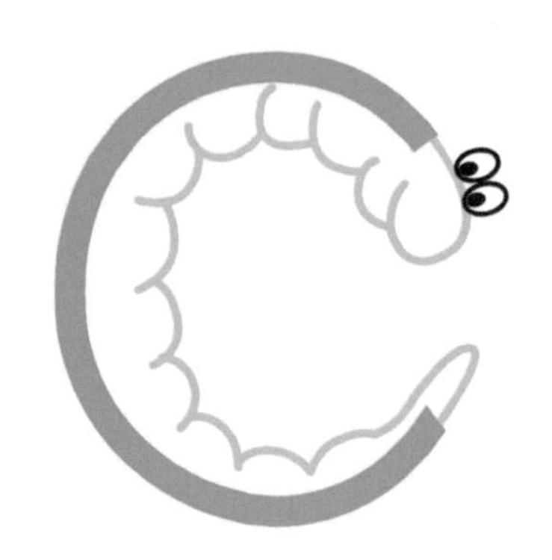

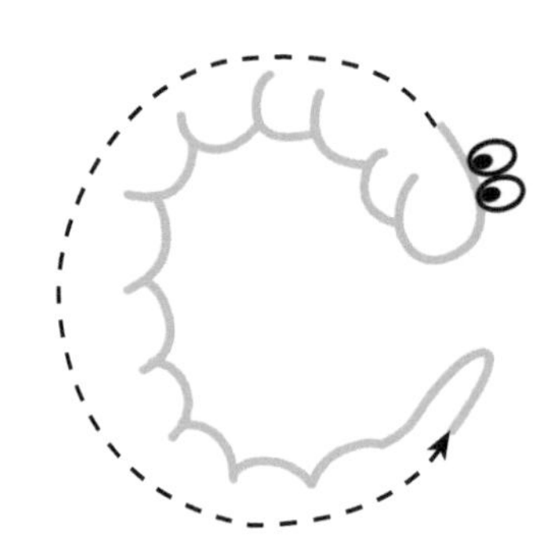

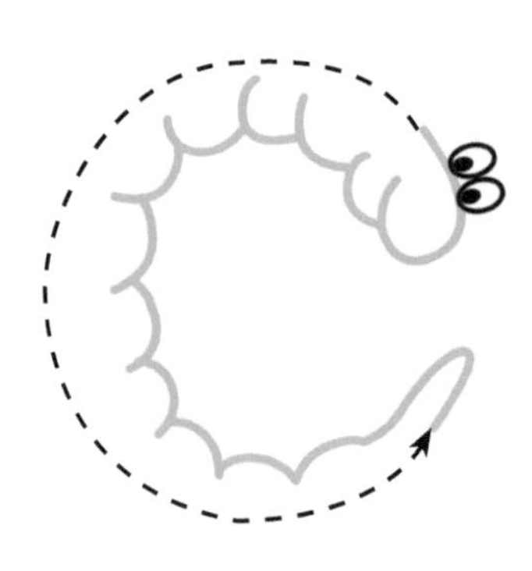

寫一寫

Trace and write

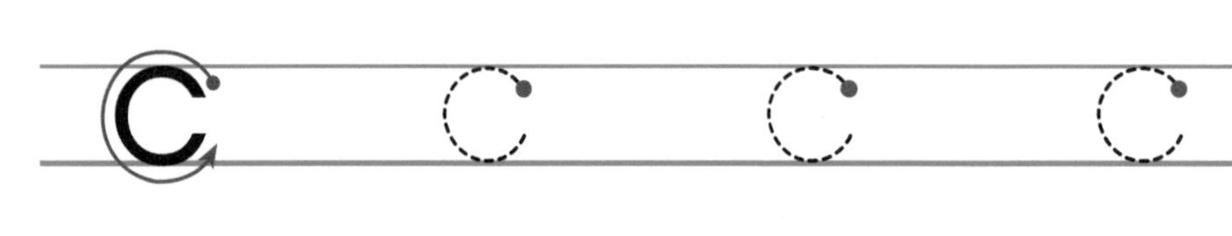

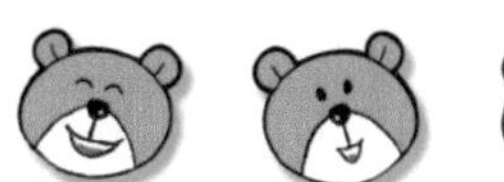

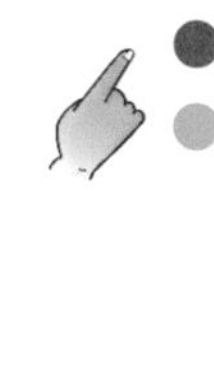
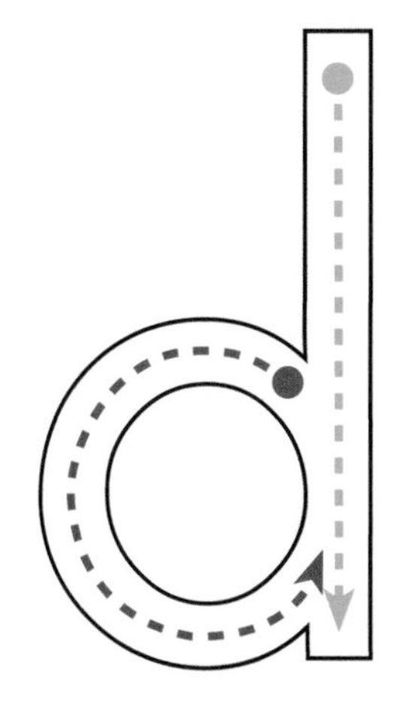

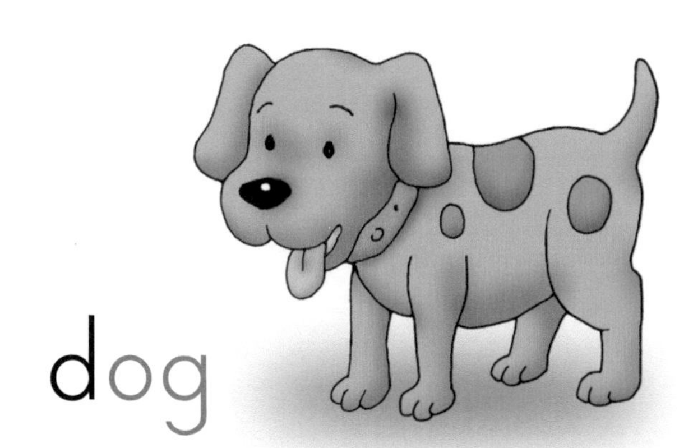

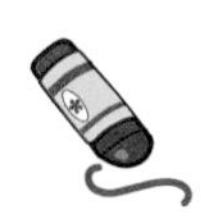

畫一畫
Trace the Lines

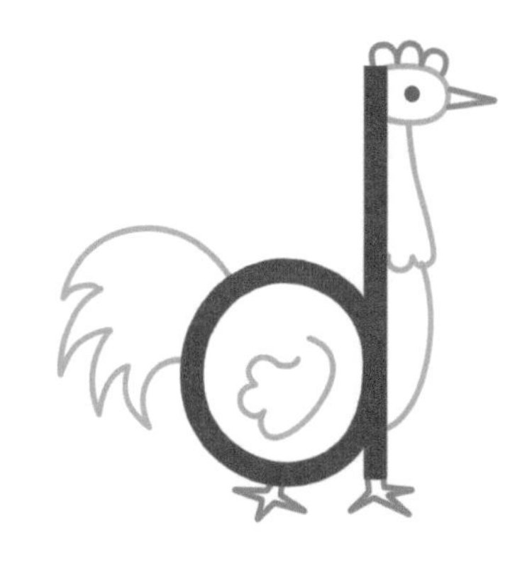
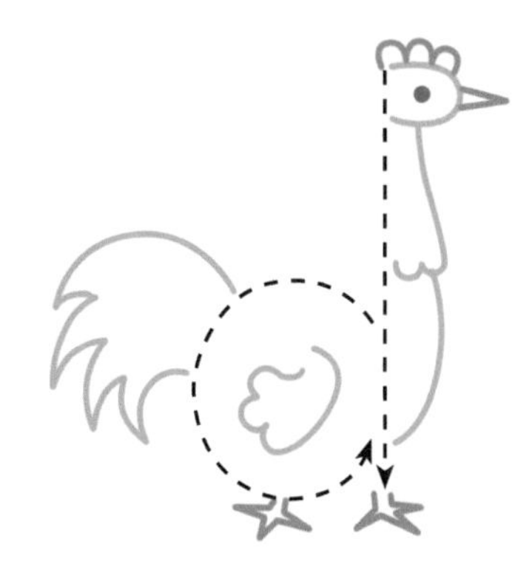
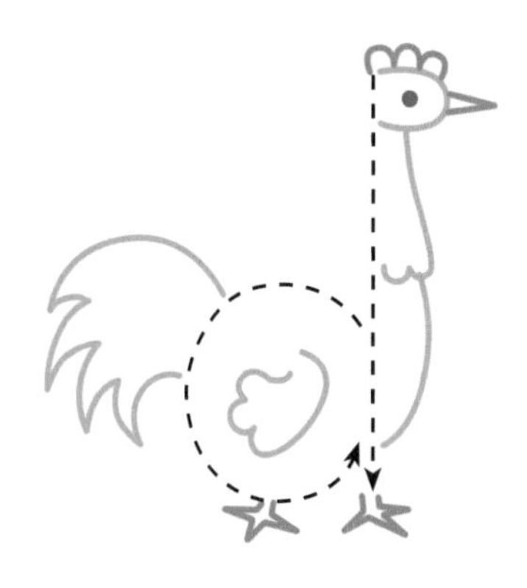

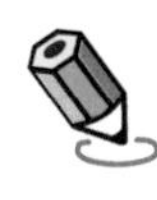

寫一寫
Trace and write

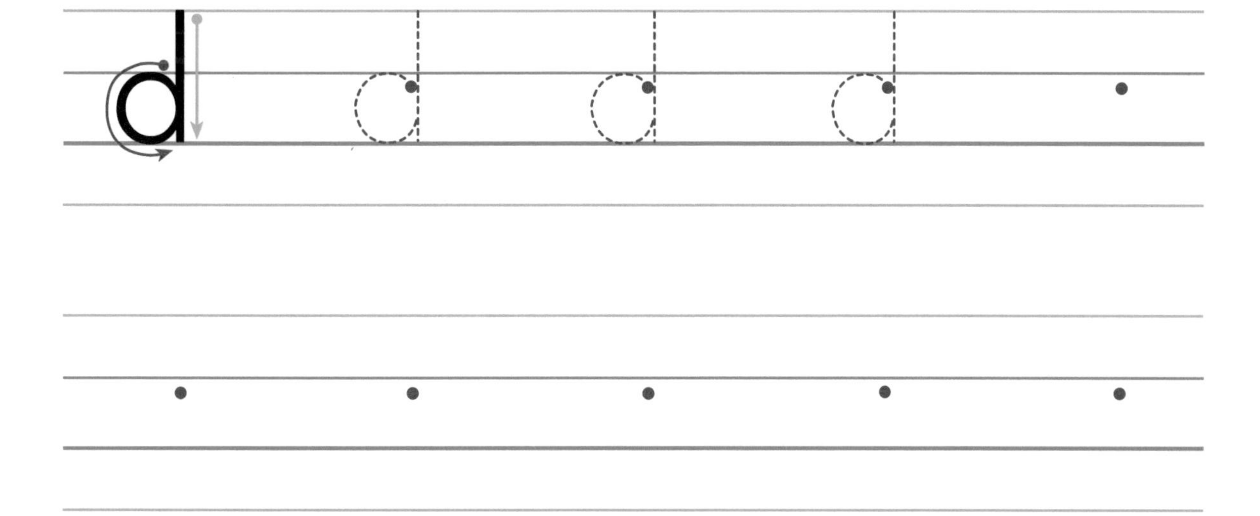

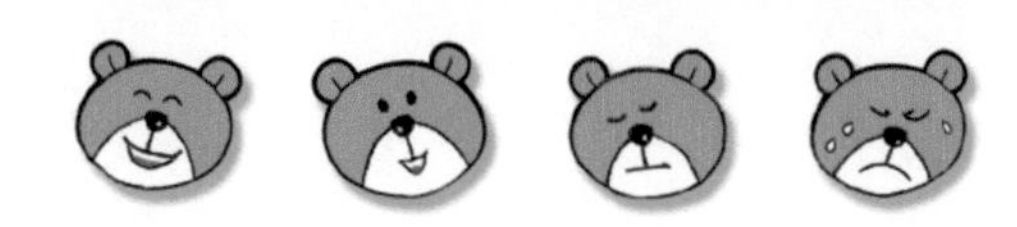

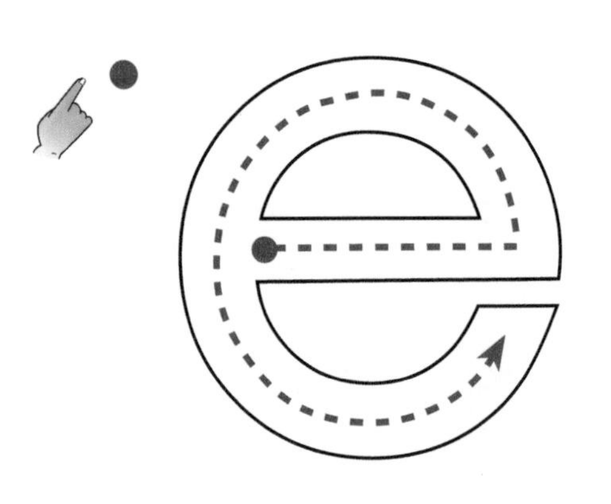

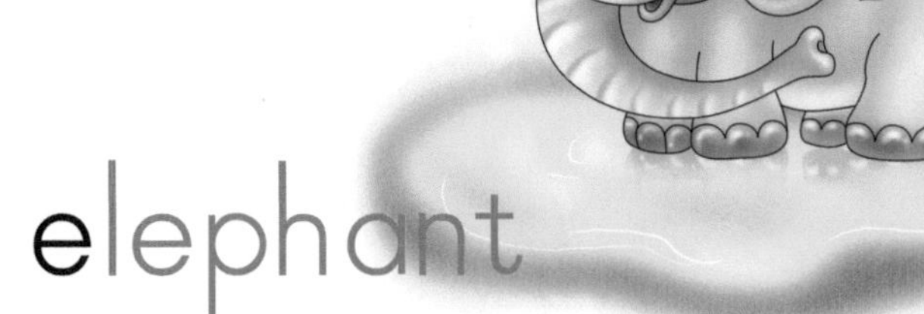

畫一畫

Trace the Lines

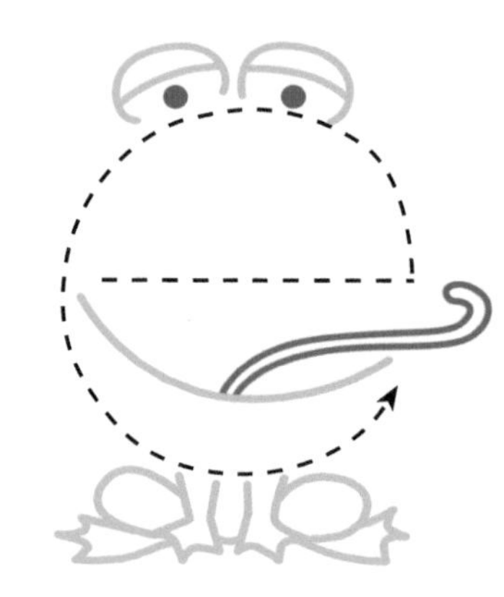
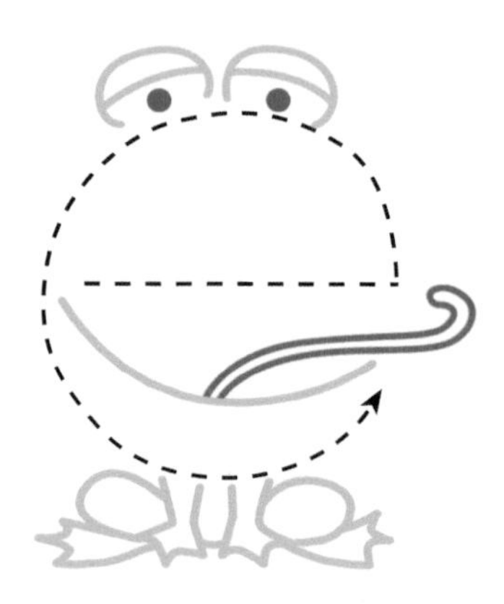

寫一寫

Trace and write

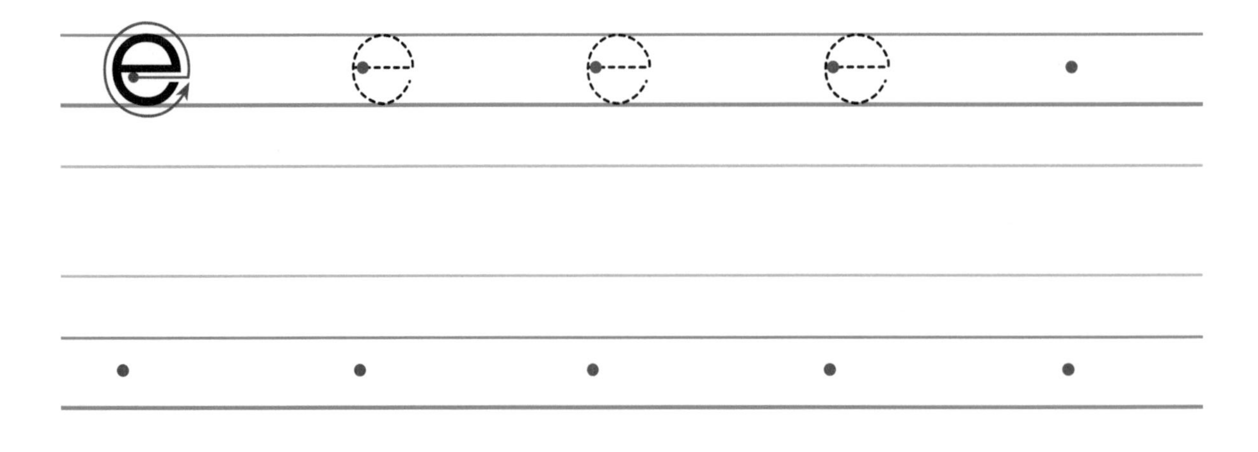

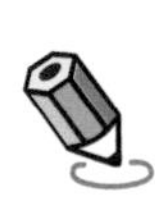

請圈出正確的圖畫。
Please circle the correct pictures.

apple	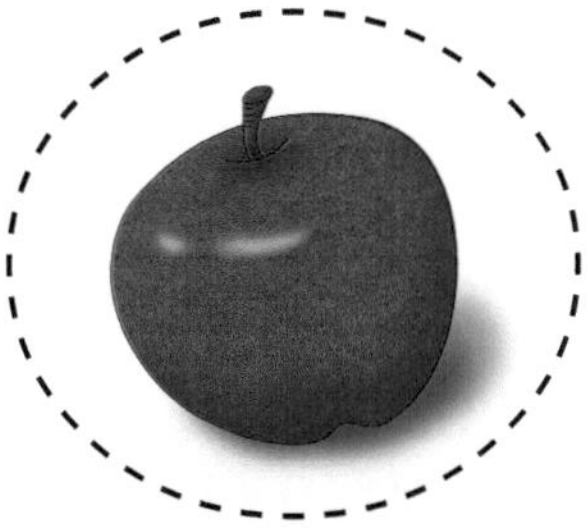 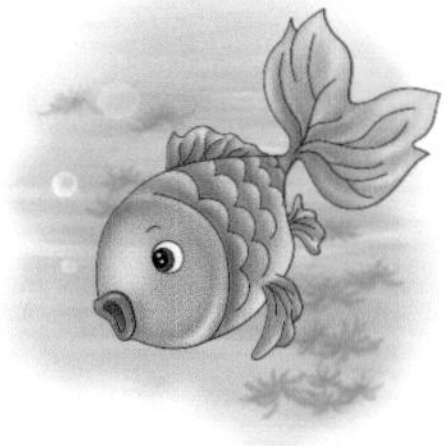
ball	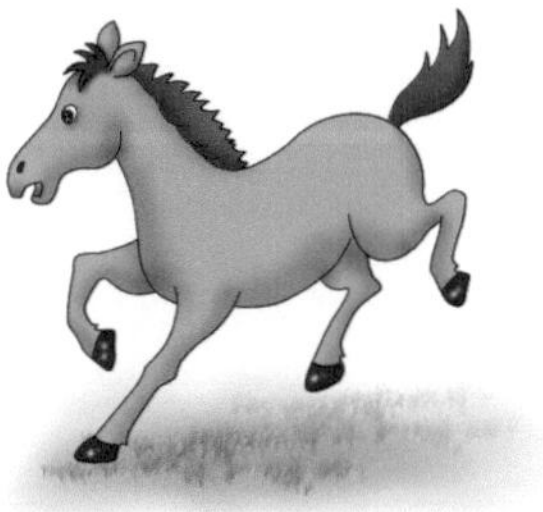 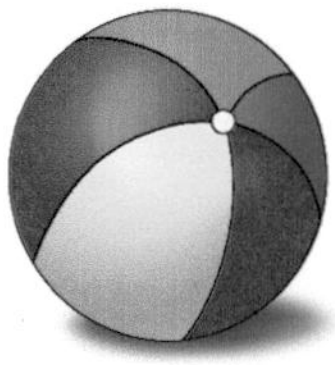
car	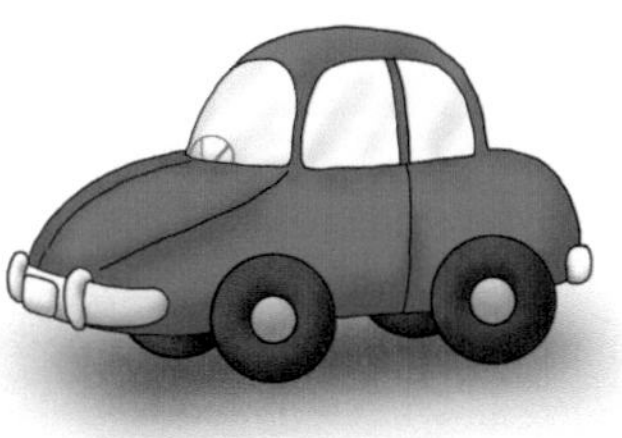 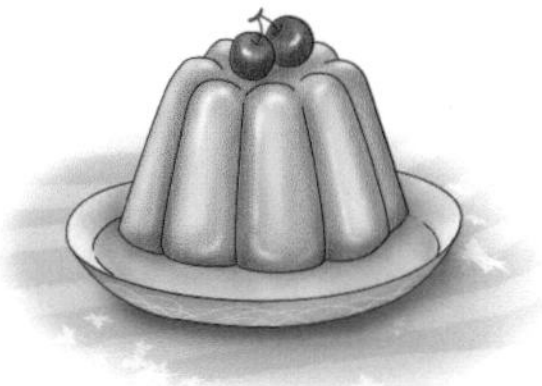
dog	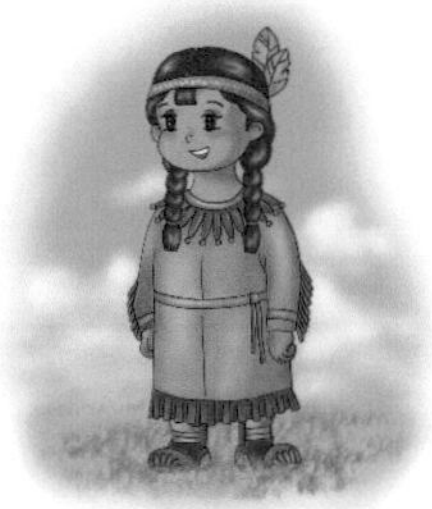 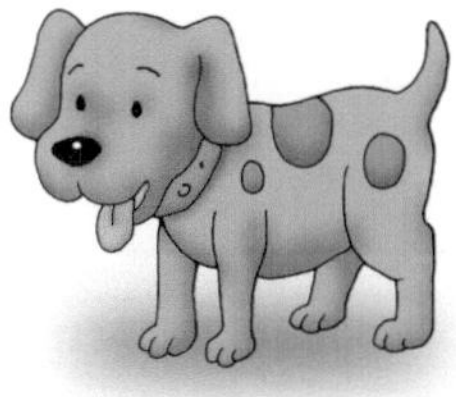
elephant	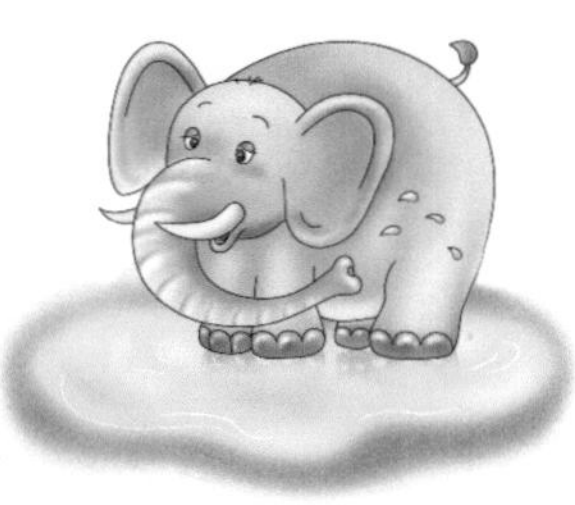 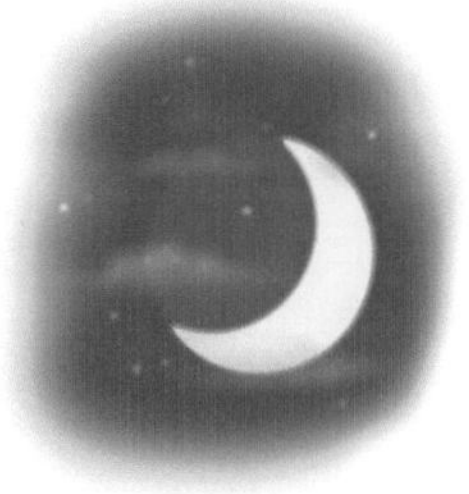

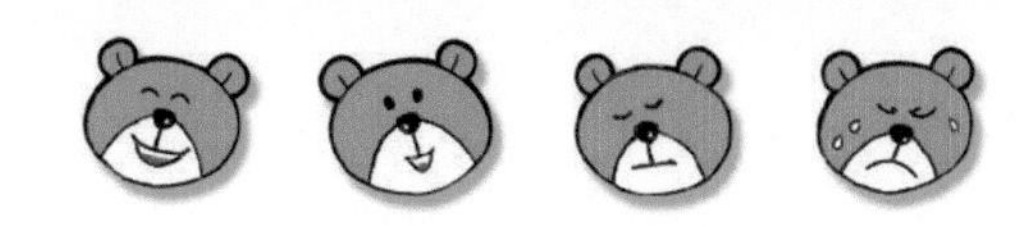

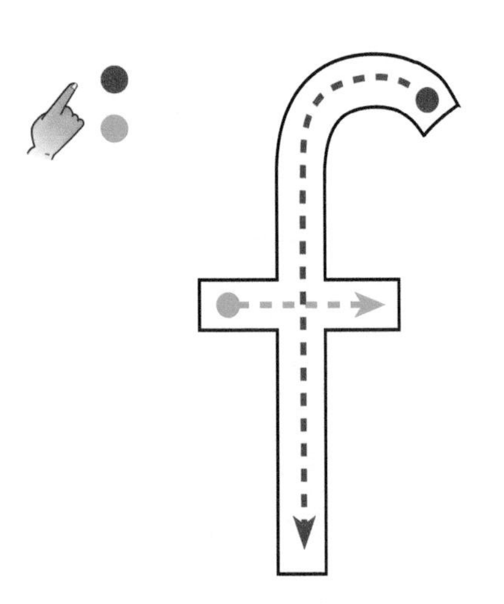

畫一畫
Trace the Lines

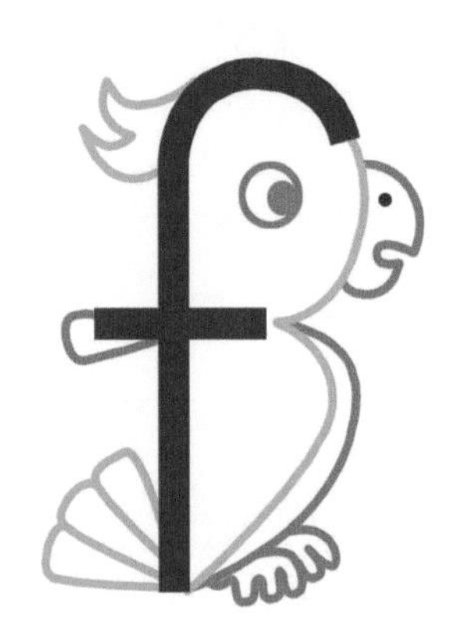

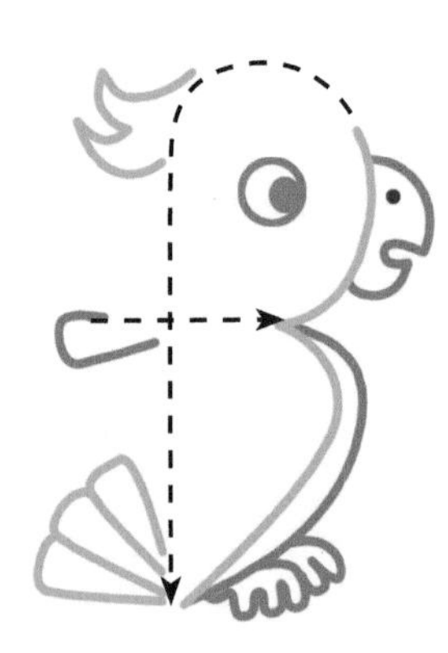

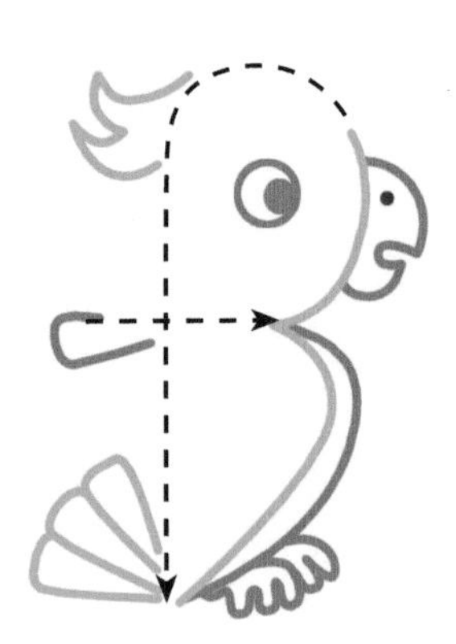

寫一寫
Trace and write

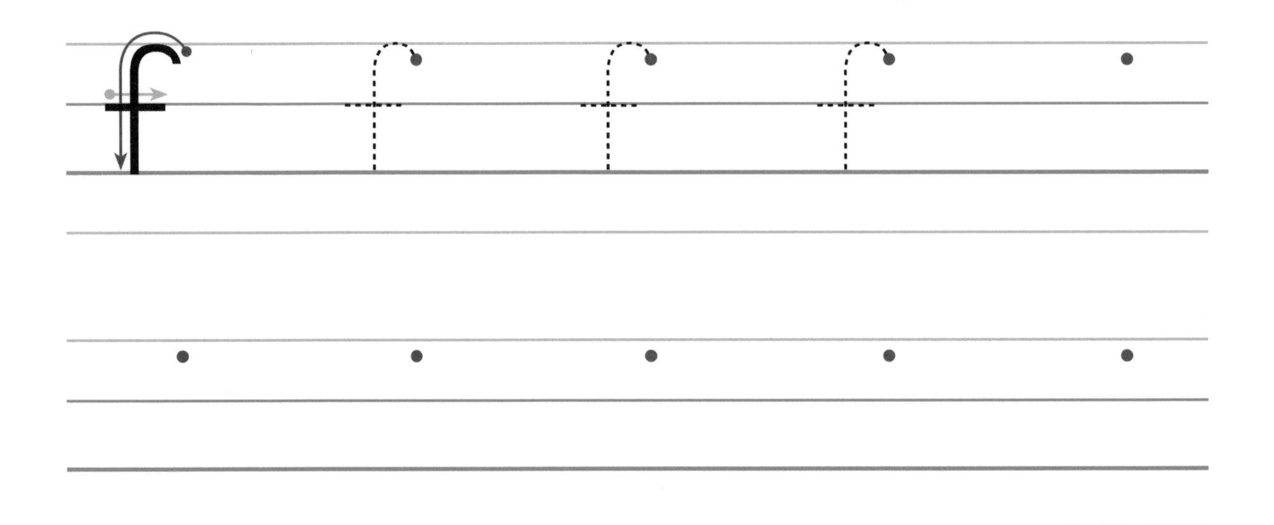

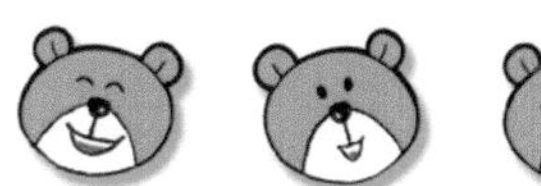
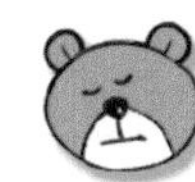

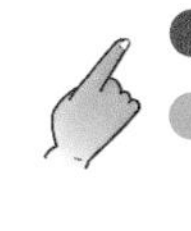
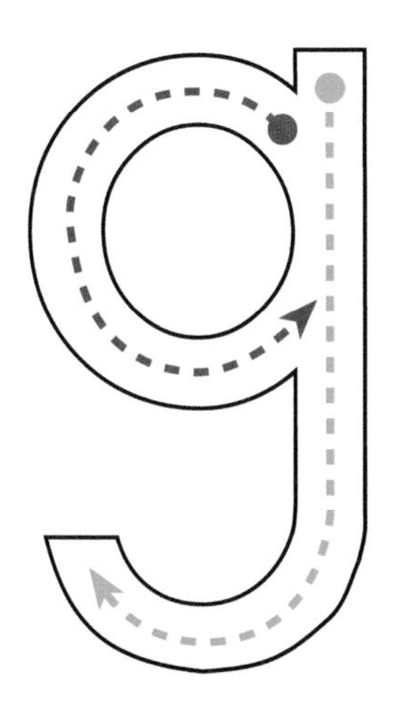

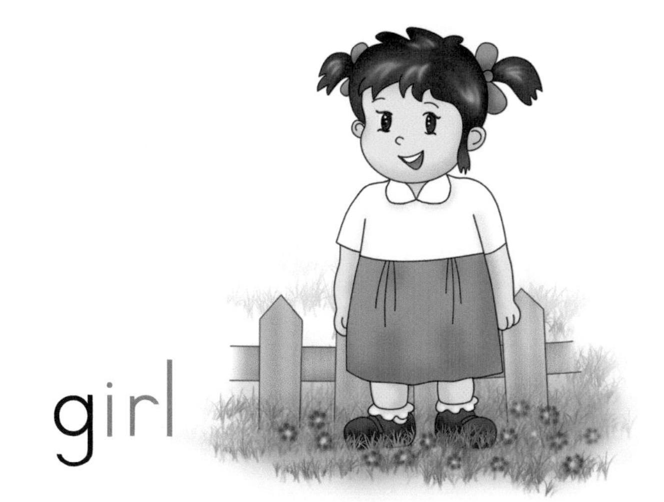

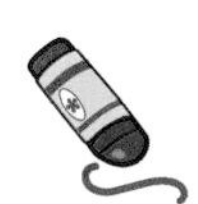

畫一畫

Trace the Lines

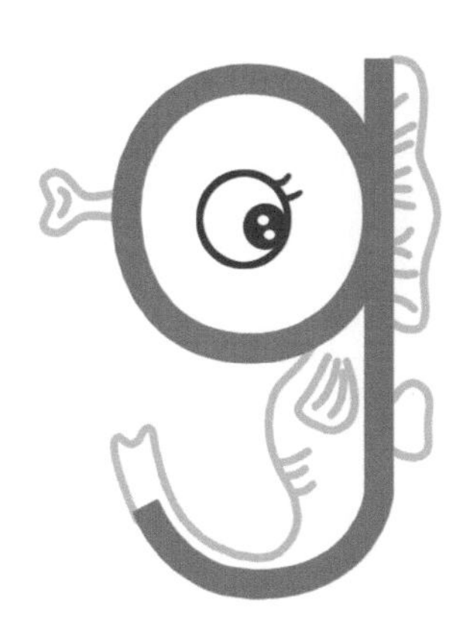
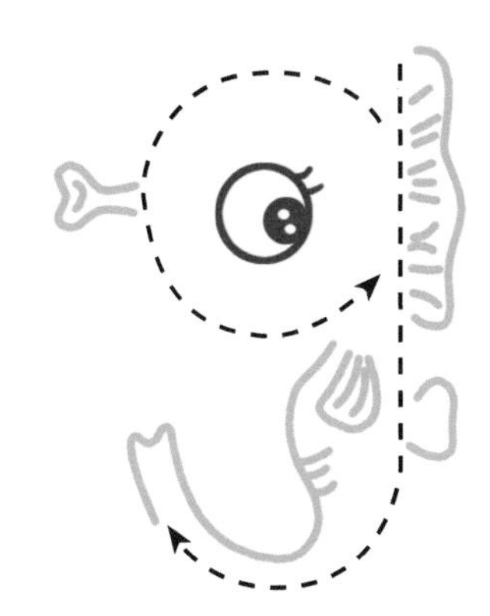
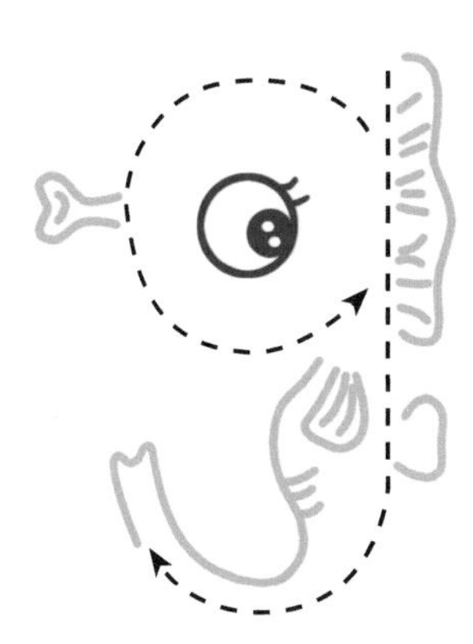

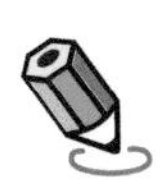

寫一寫

Trace and write

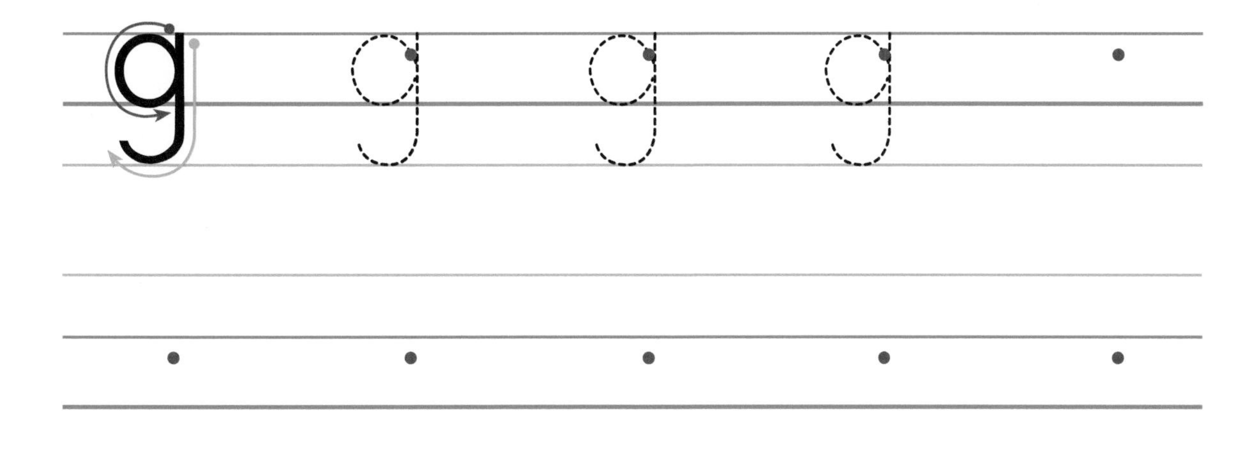

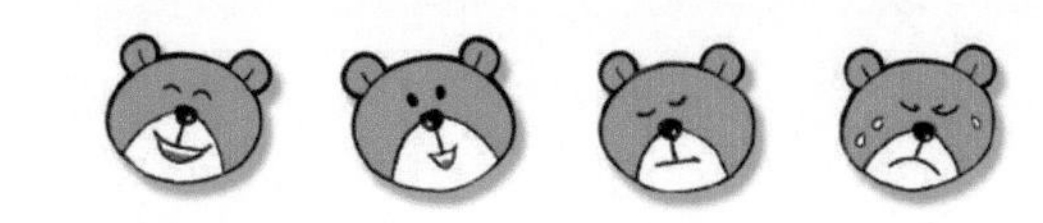

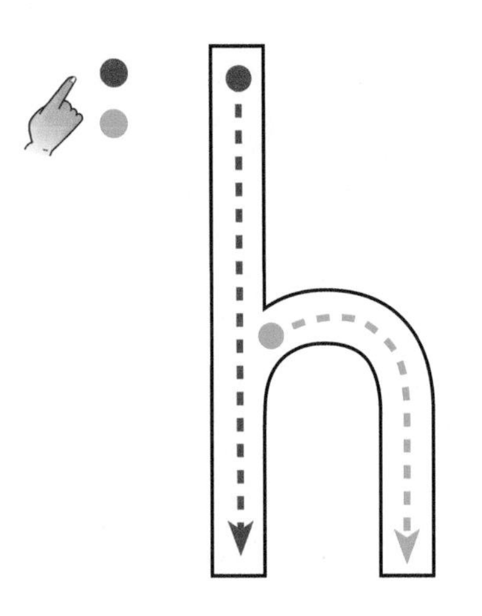

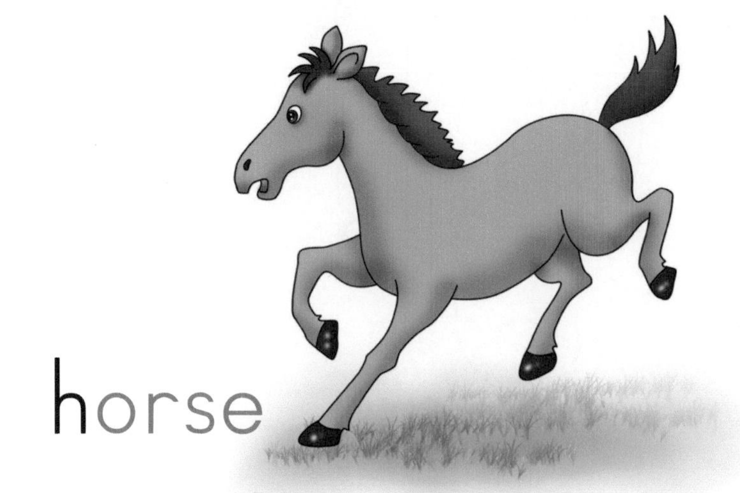

畫一畫
Trace the Lines

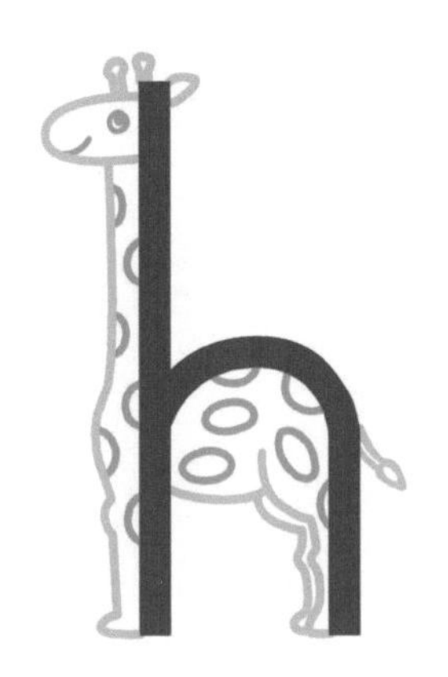

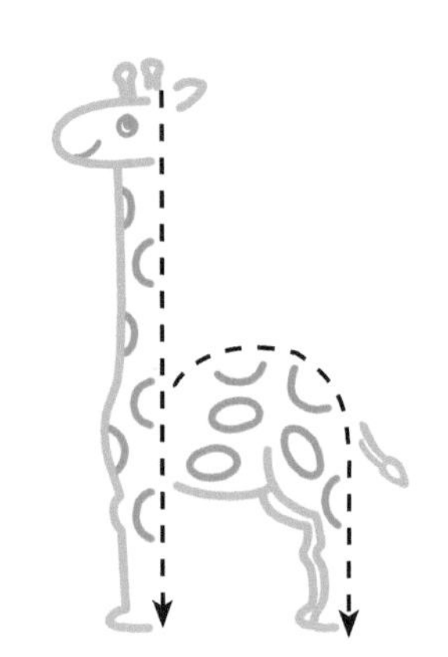

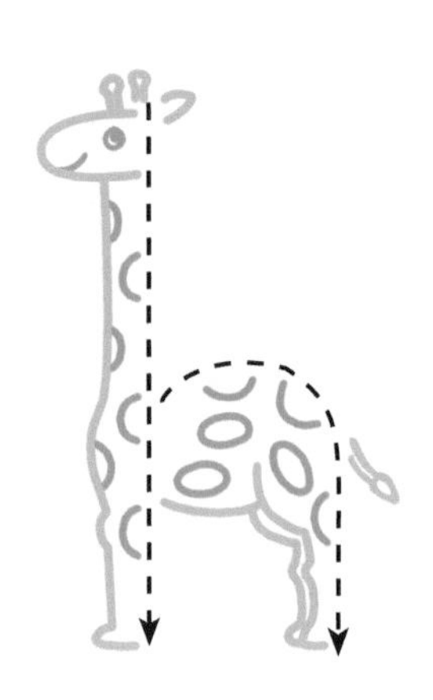

寫一寫
Trace and write

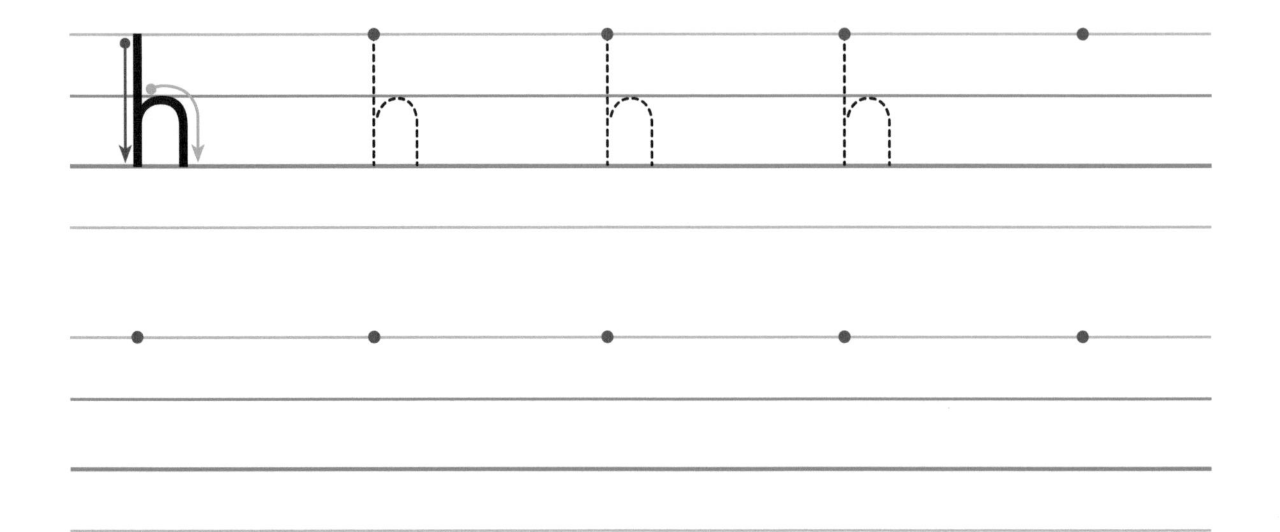

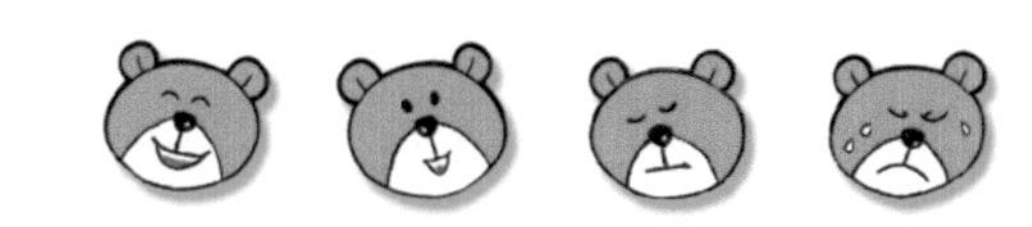

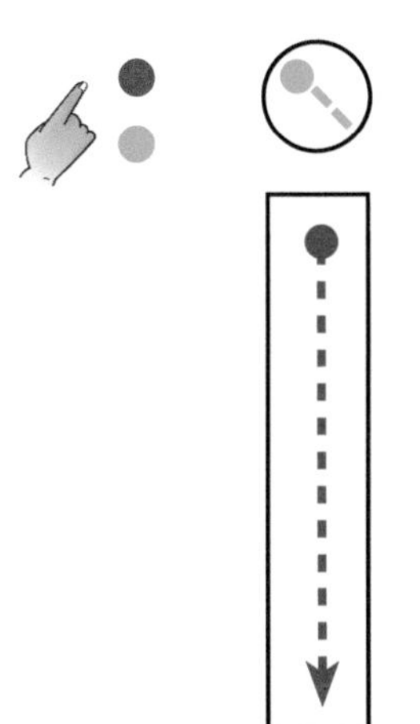

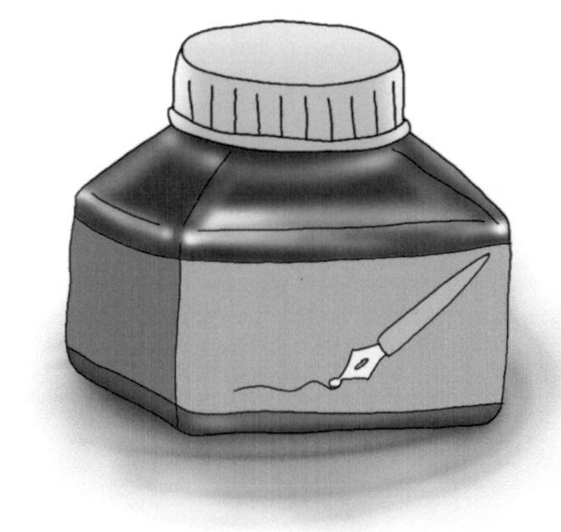

ink

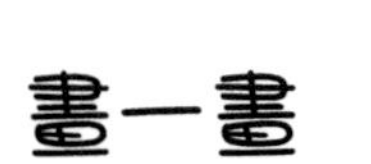

畫一畫
Trace the Lines

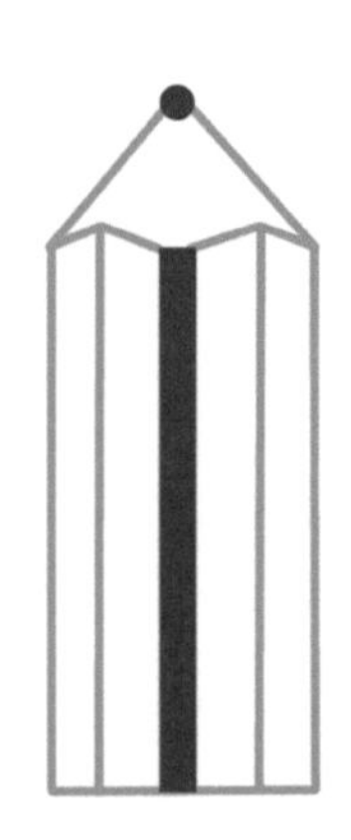

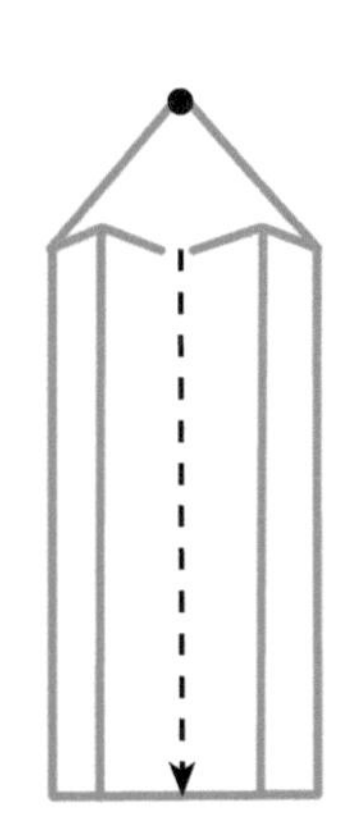

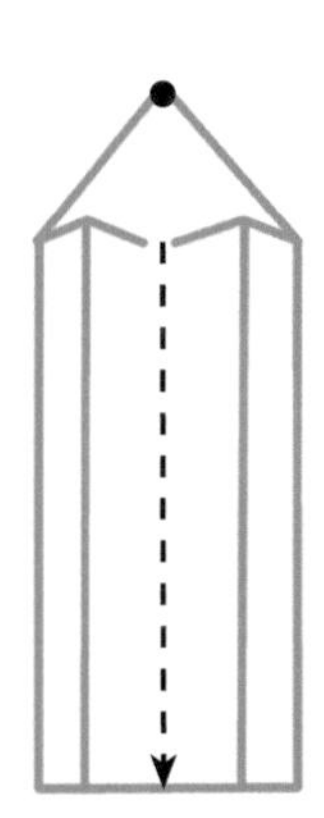

寫一寫
Trace and write

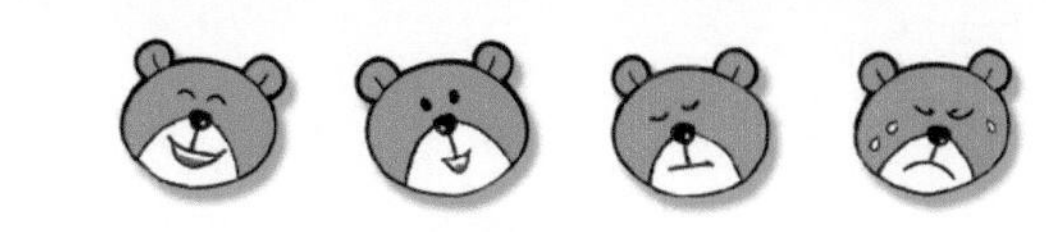

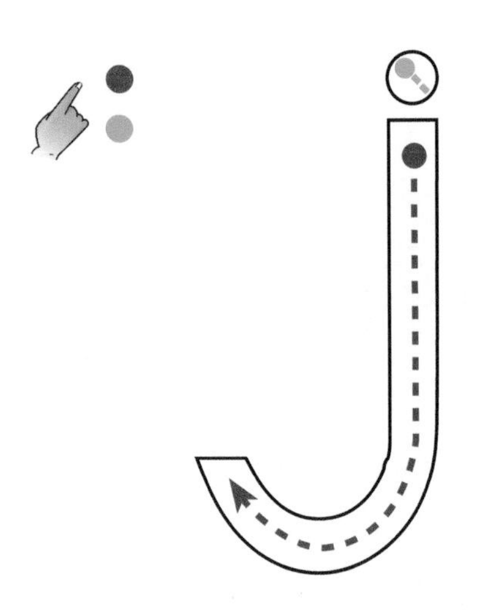

jelly

畫一畫
Trace the Lines

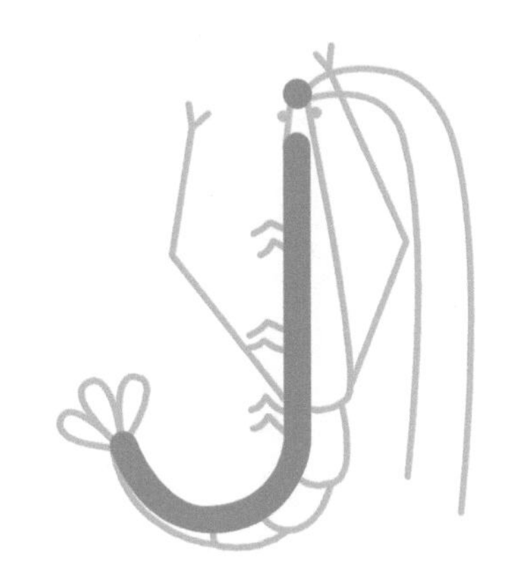

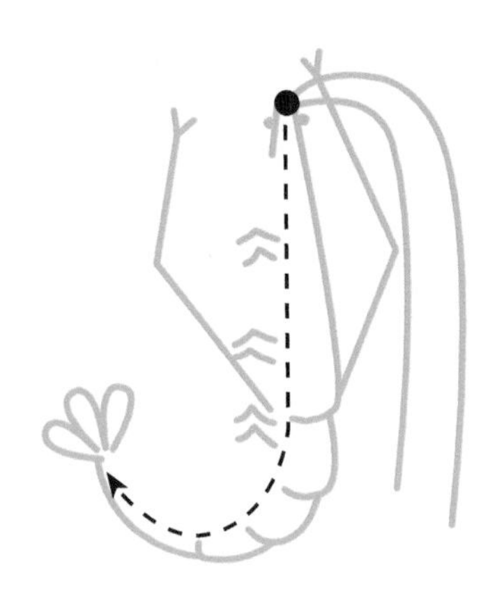

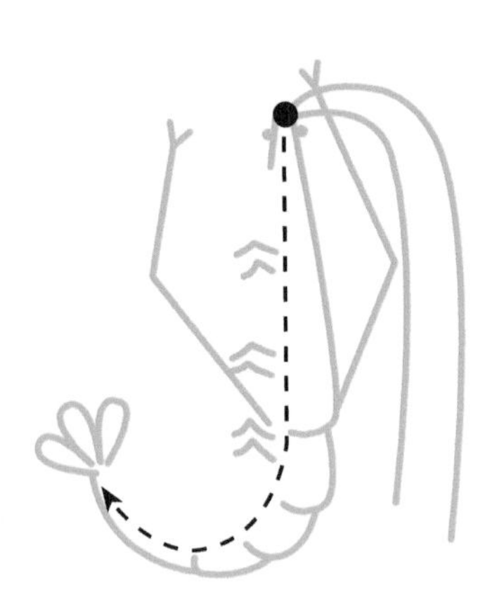

寫一寫
Trace and write

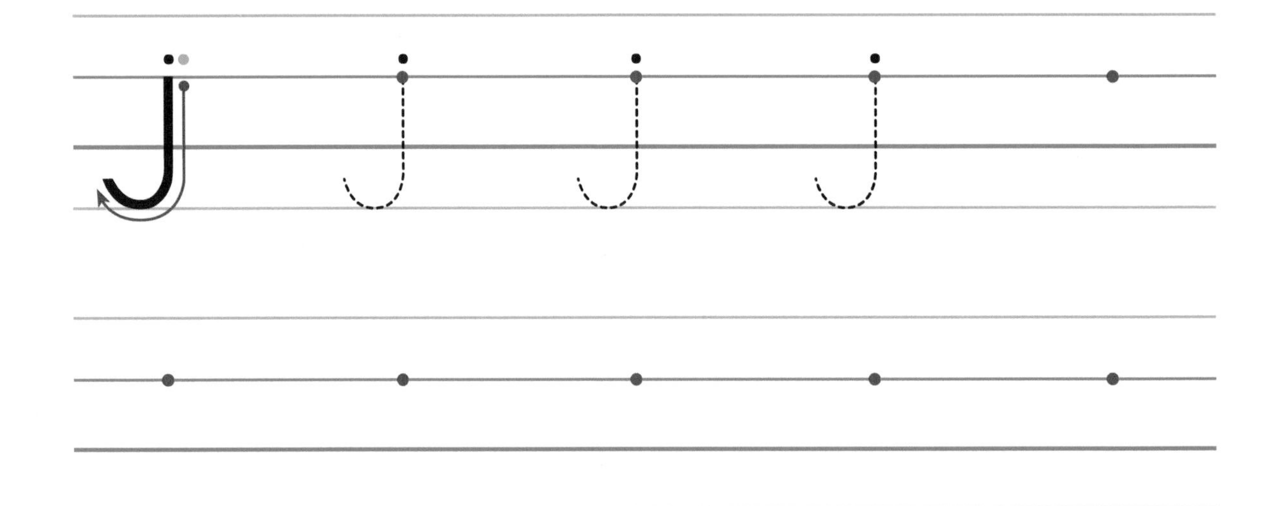

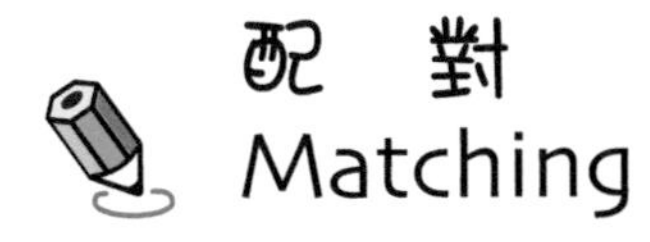

配對
Matching

fish  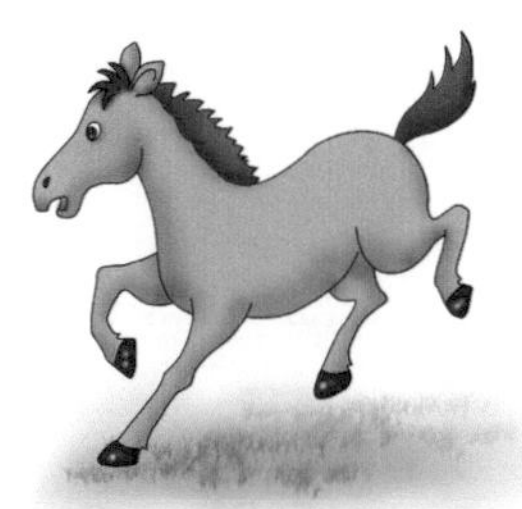

girl 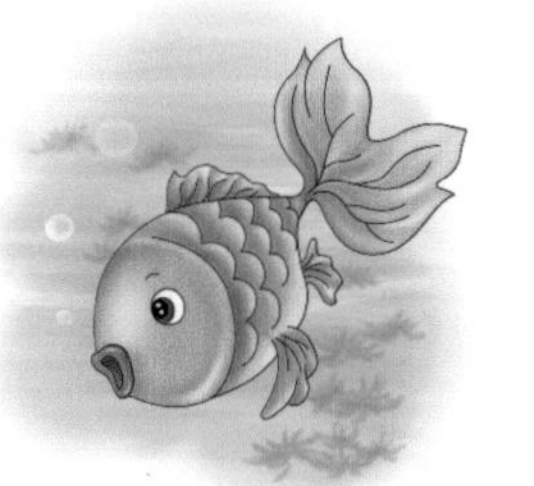

horse  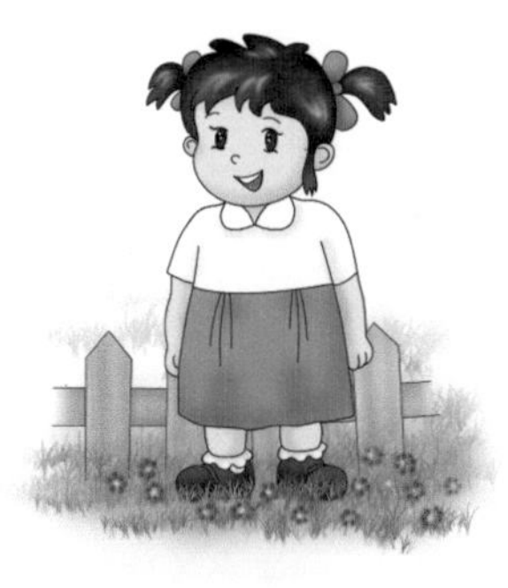

ink  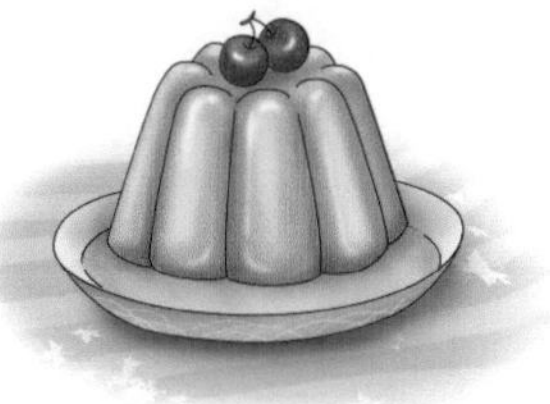

jelly  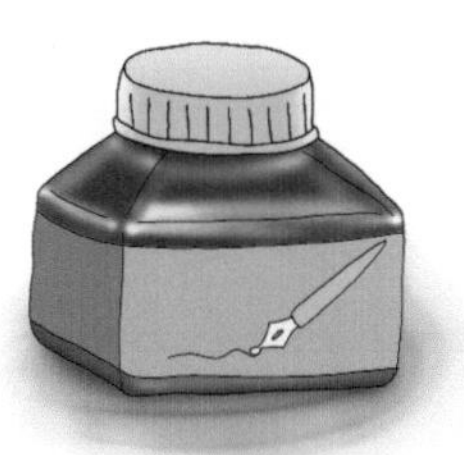

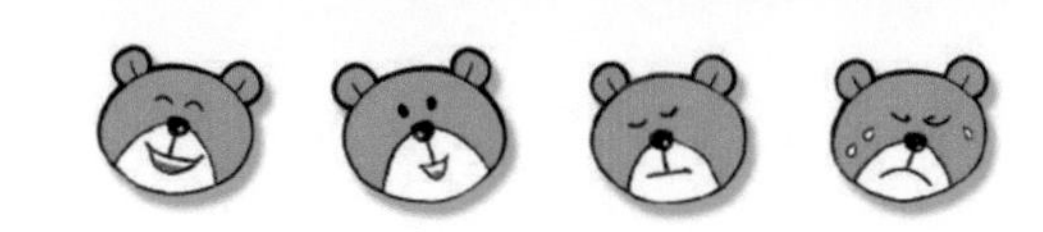

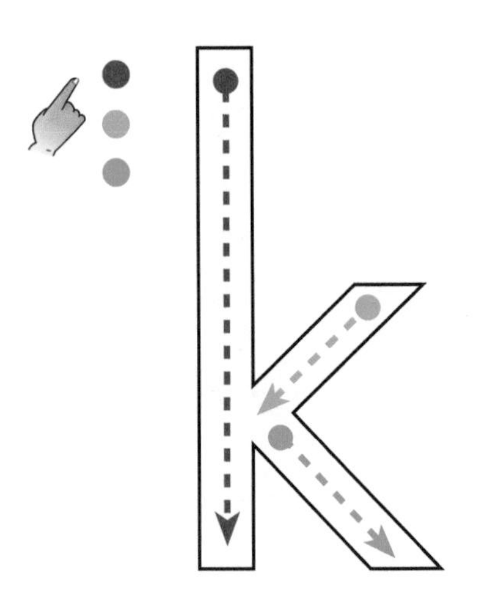

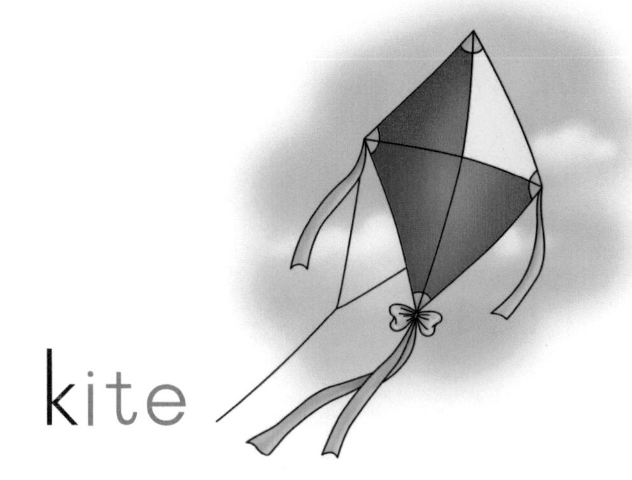

畫一畫

Trace the Lines

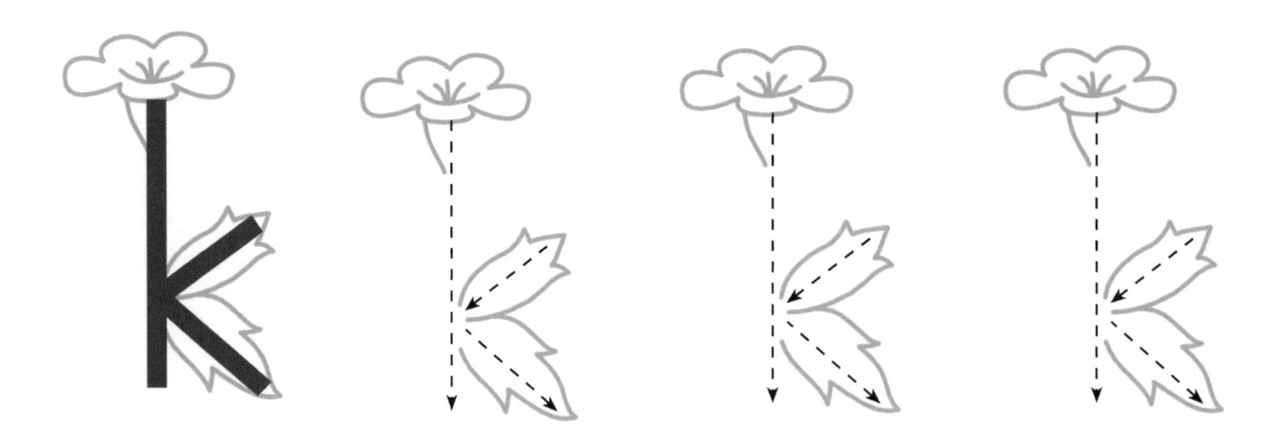

寫一寫

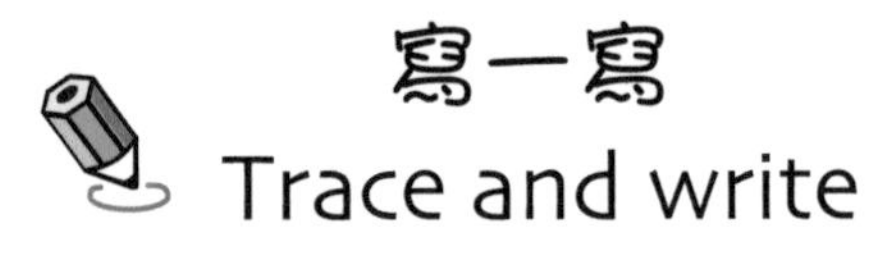
Trace and write

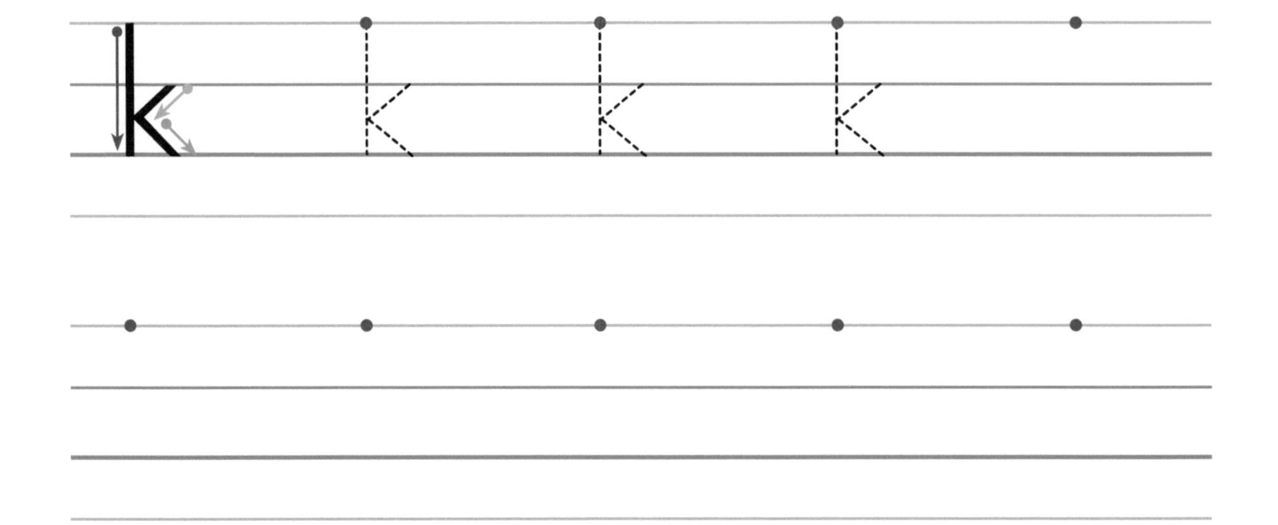

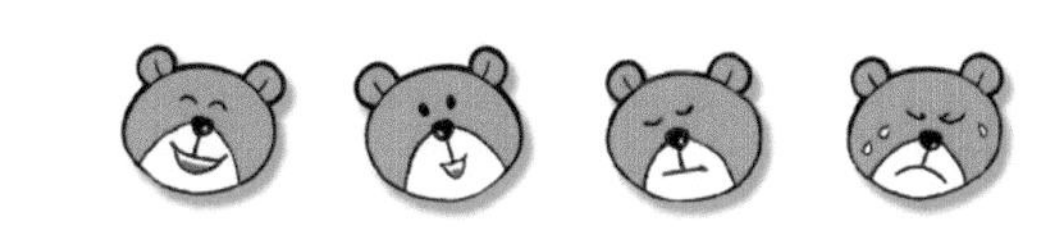

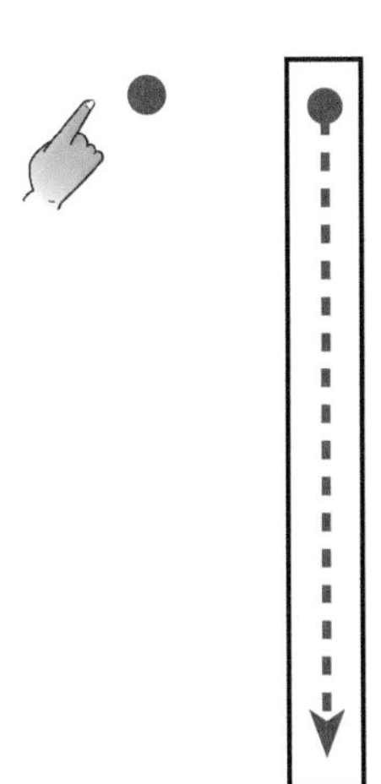

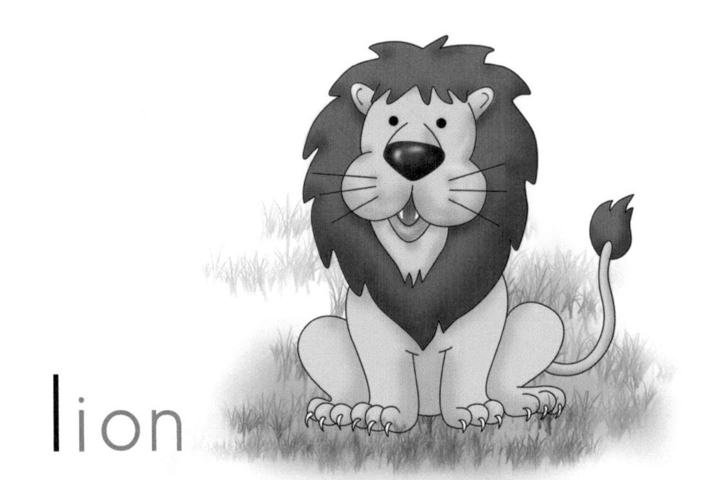

畫一畫
Trace the Lines

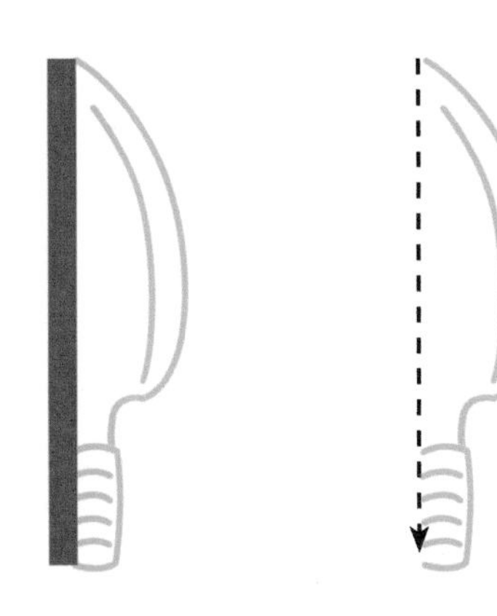

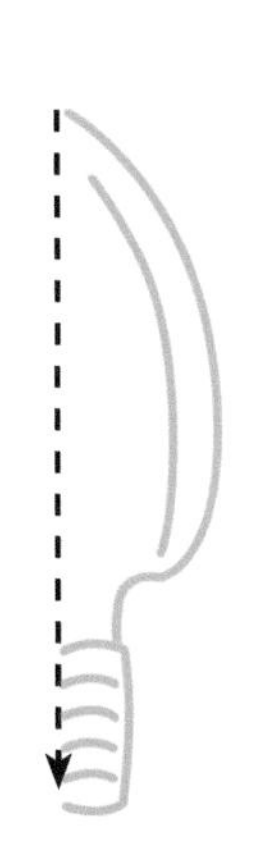

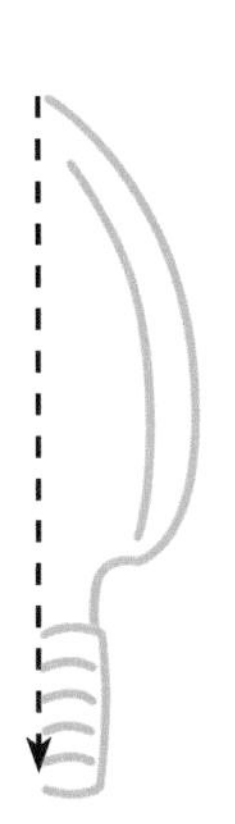

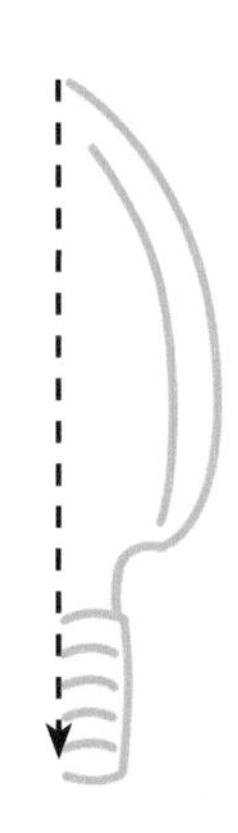

寫一寫
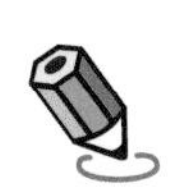

Trace and write

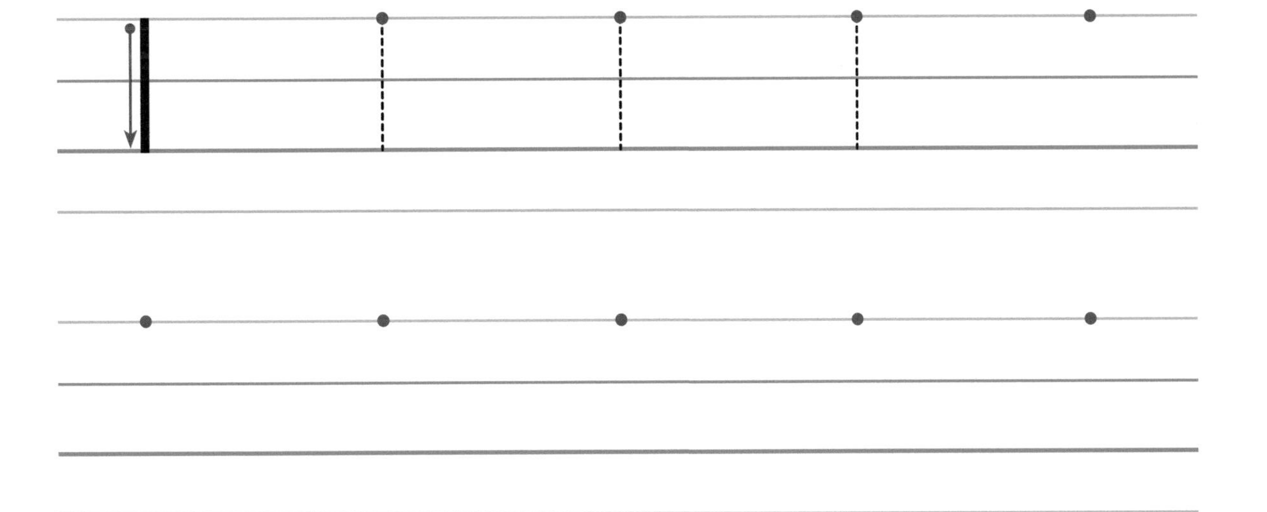

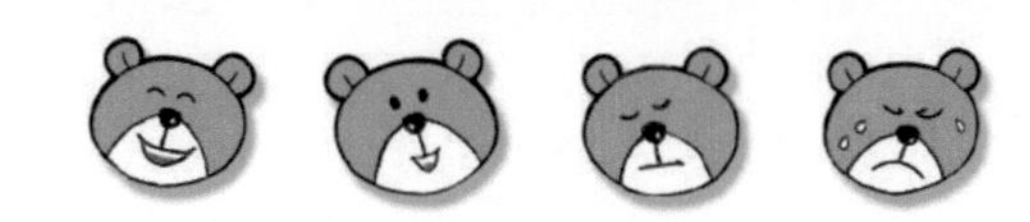

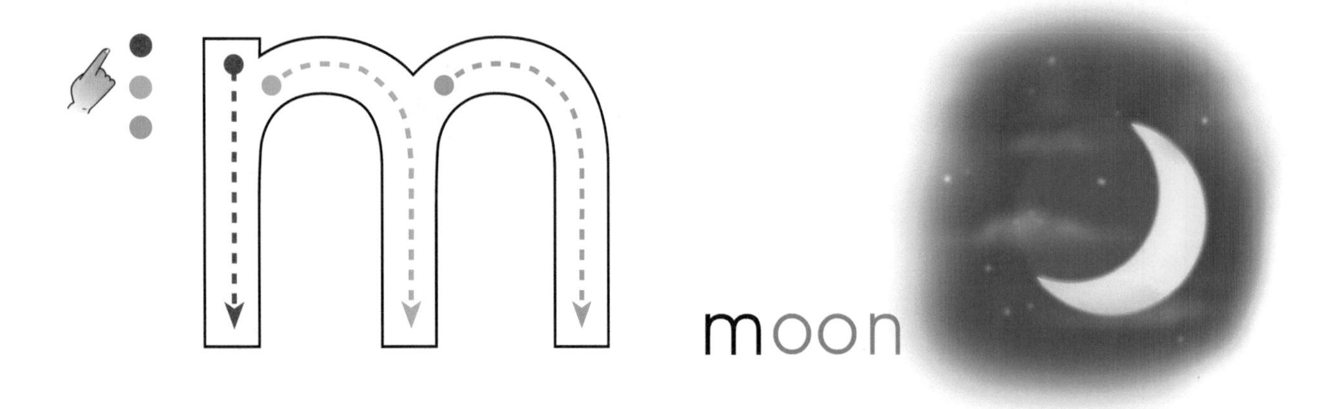
moon

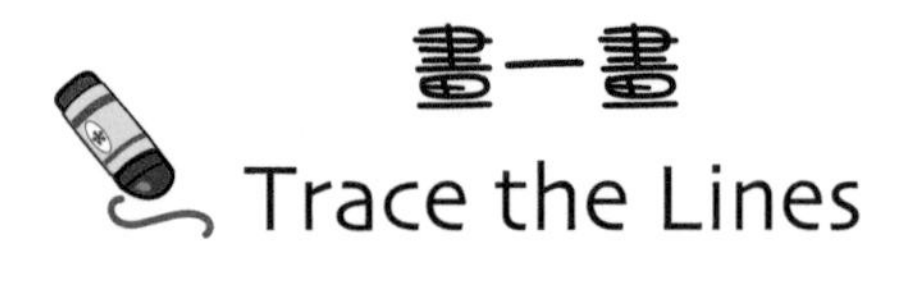
畫一畫
Trace the Lines

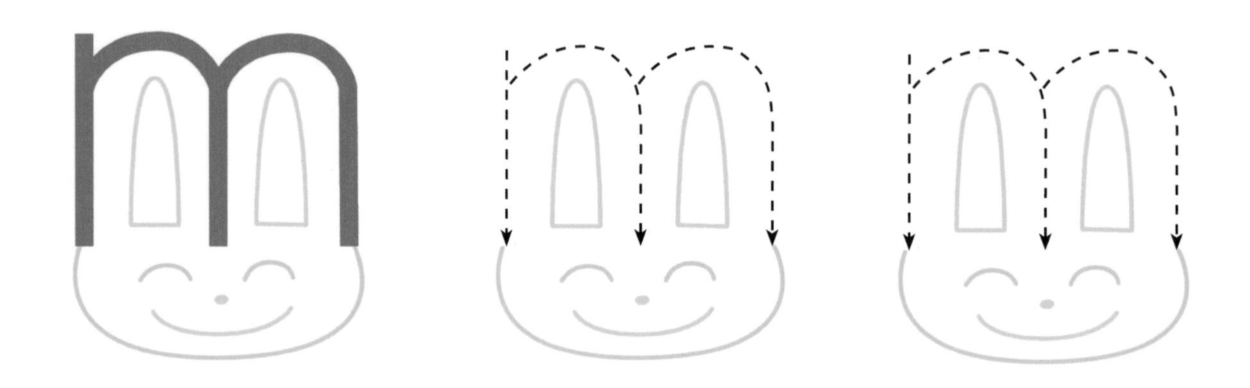

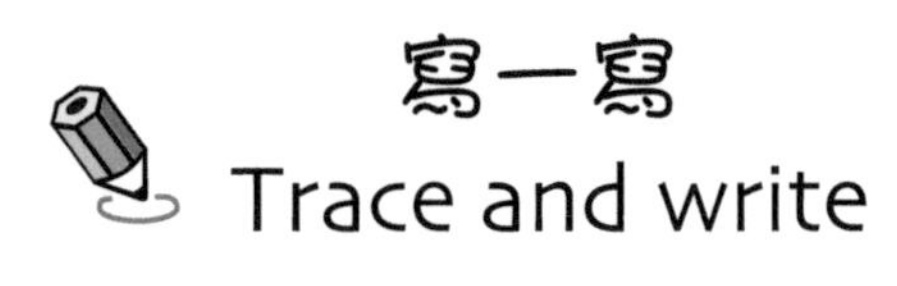
寫一寫
Trace and write

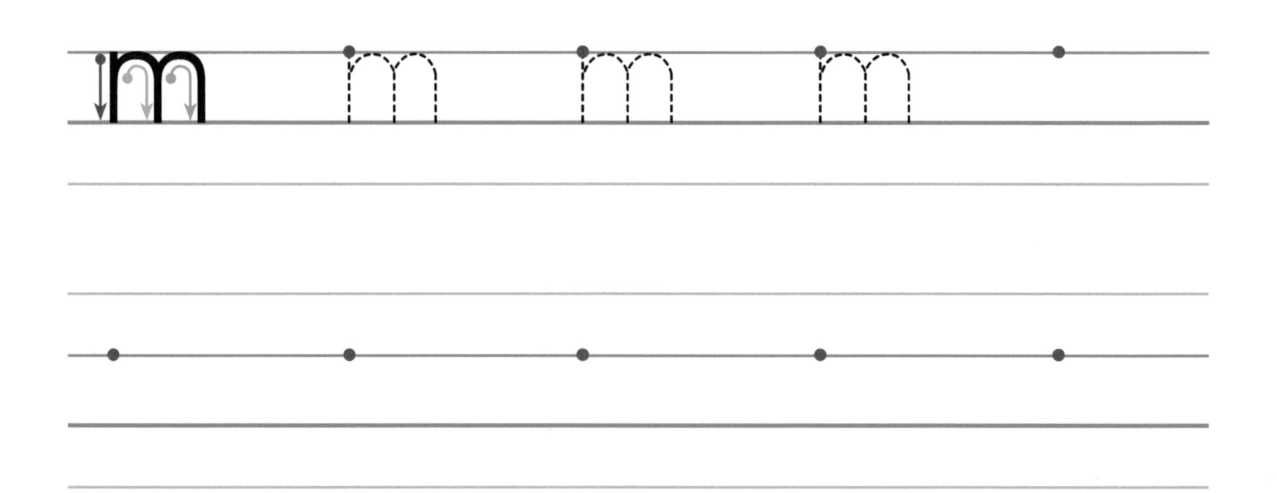

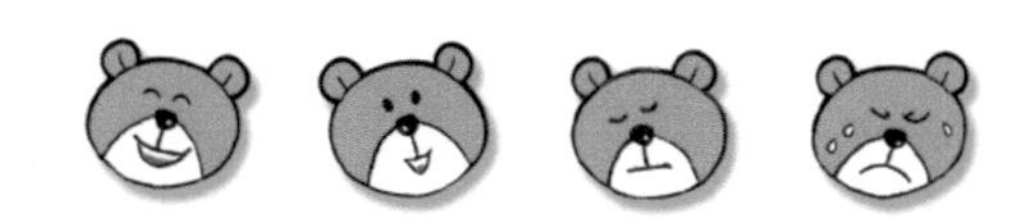

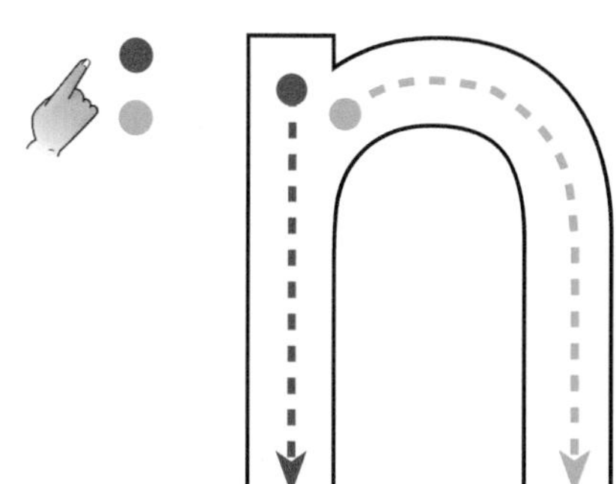

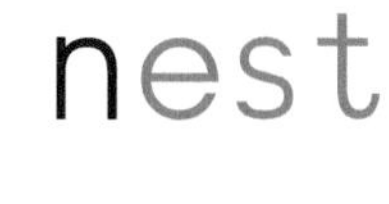

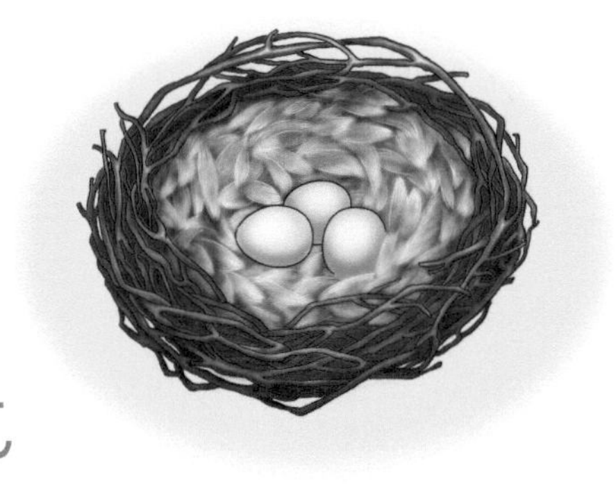

nest

畫一畫

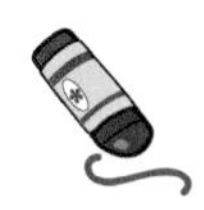

Trace the Lines

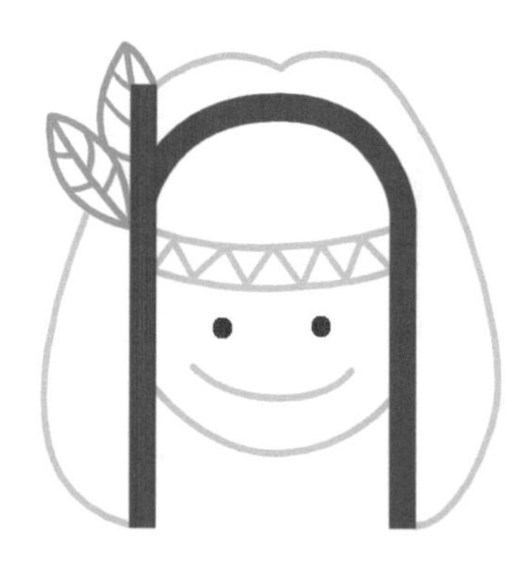

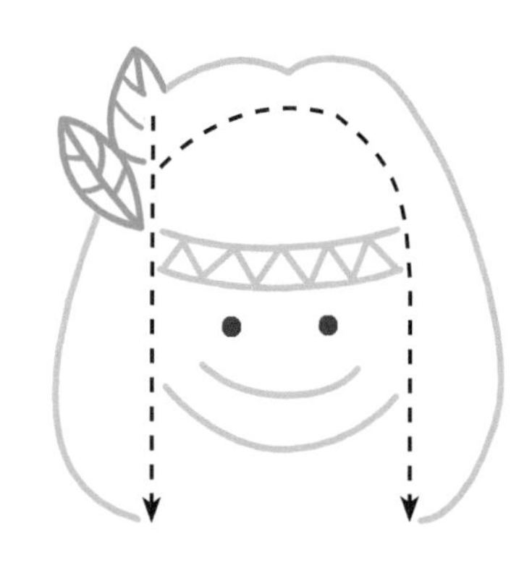

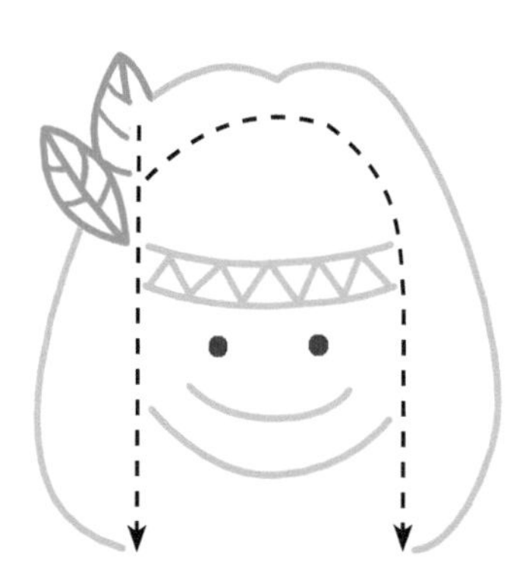

寫一寫

Trace and write

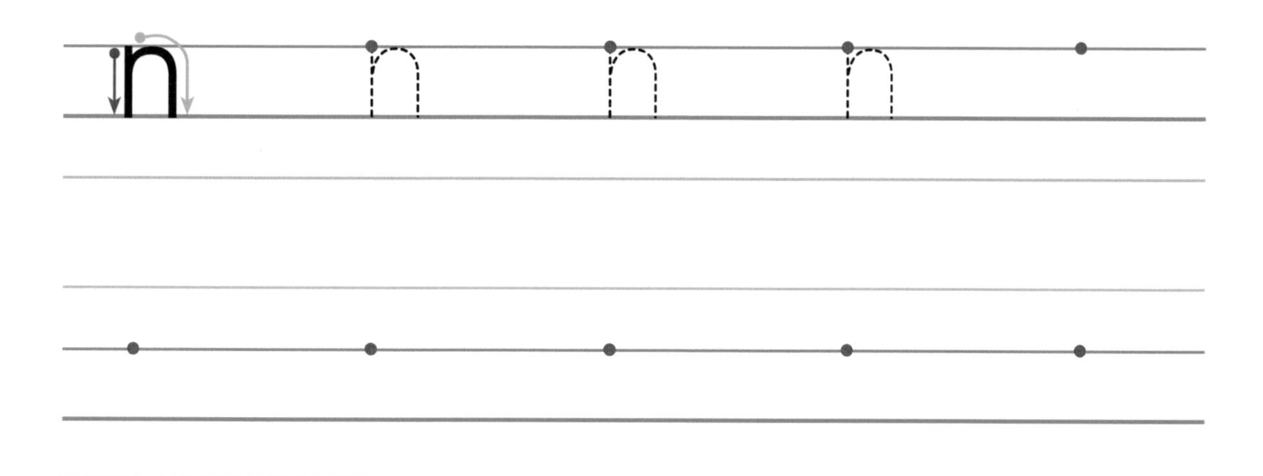

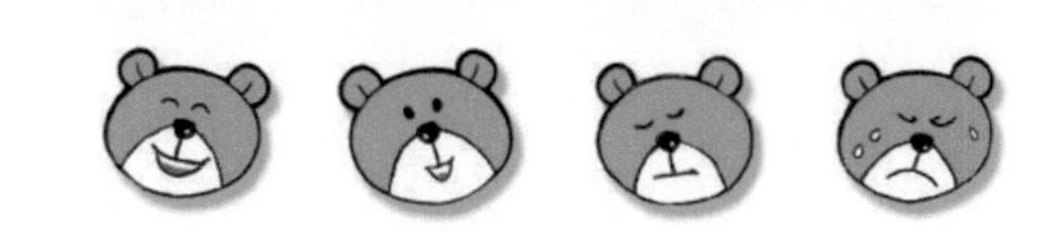

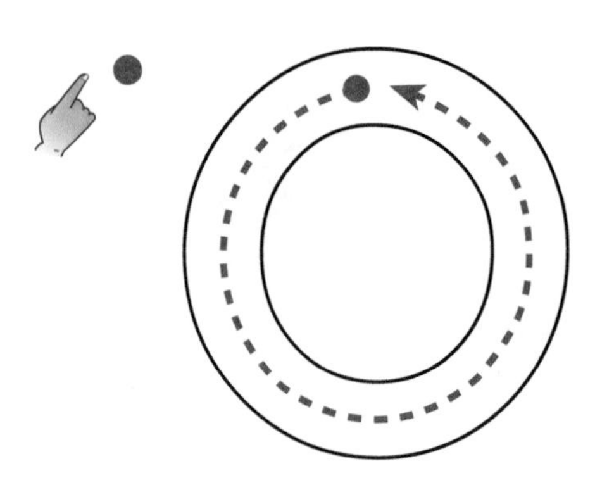

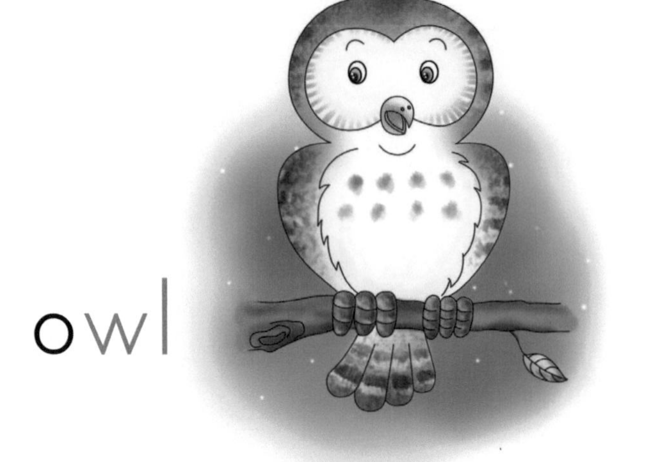

畫一畫
Trace the Lines

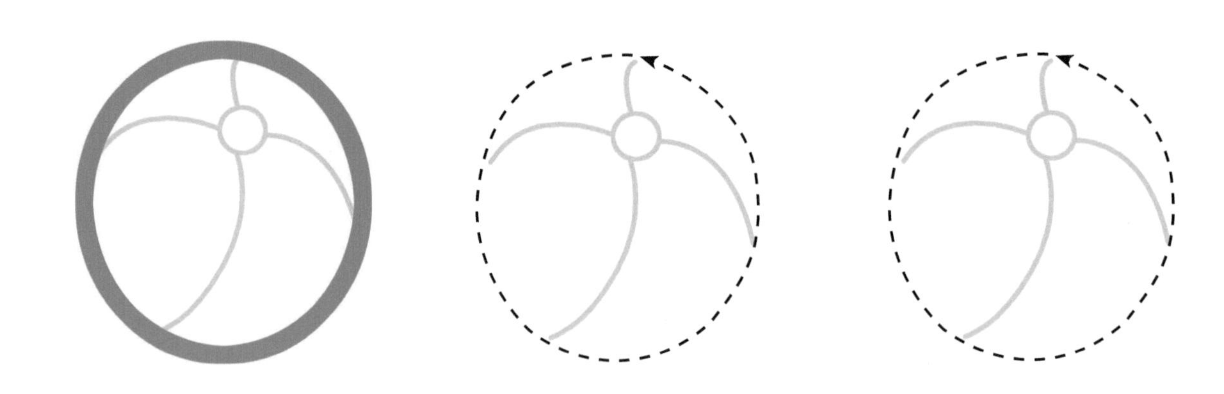

寫一寫
Trace and write

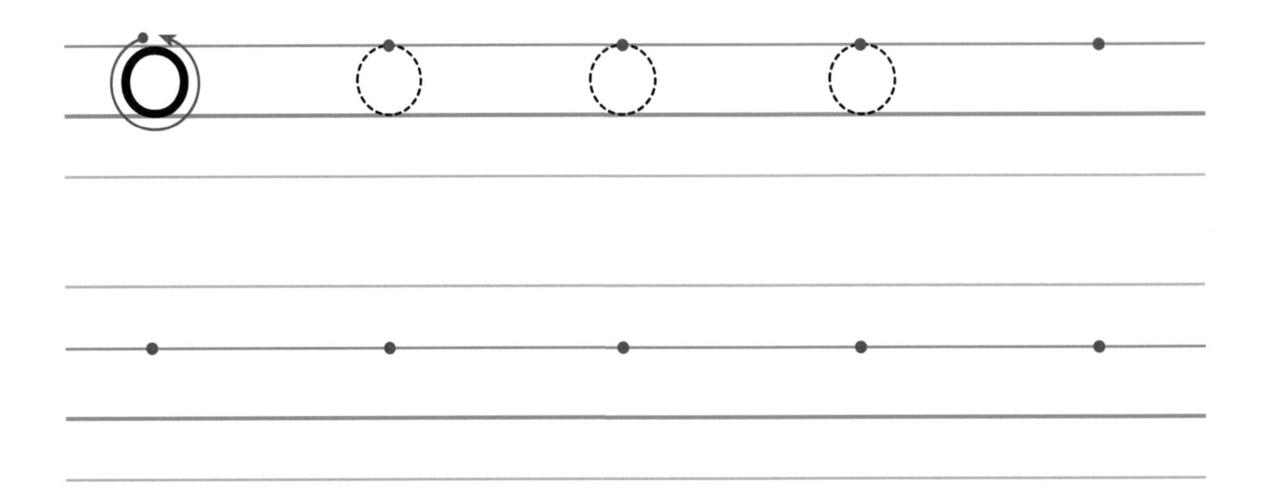

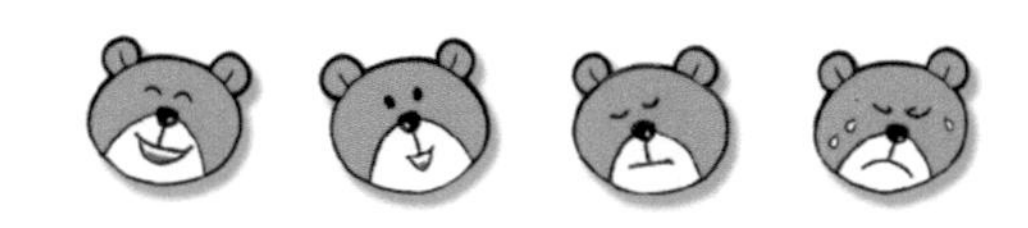

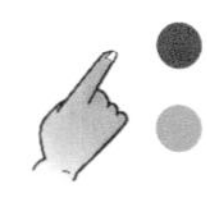
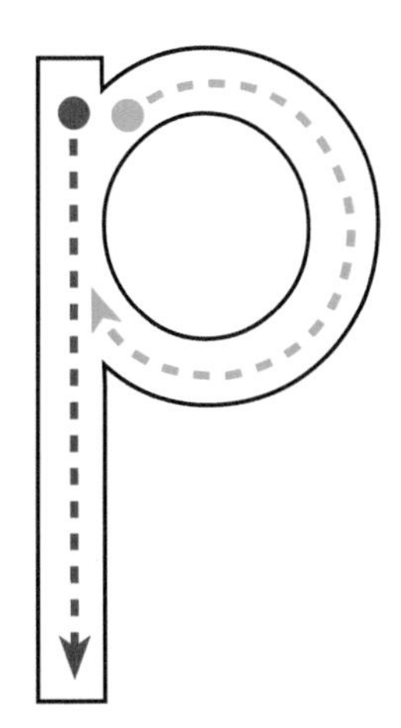

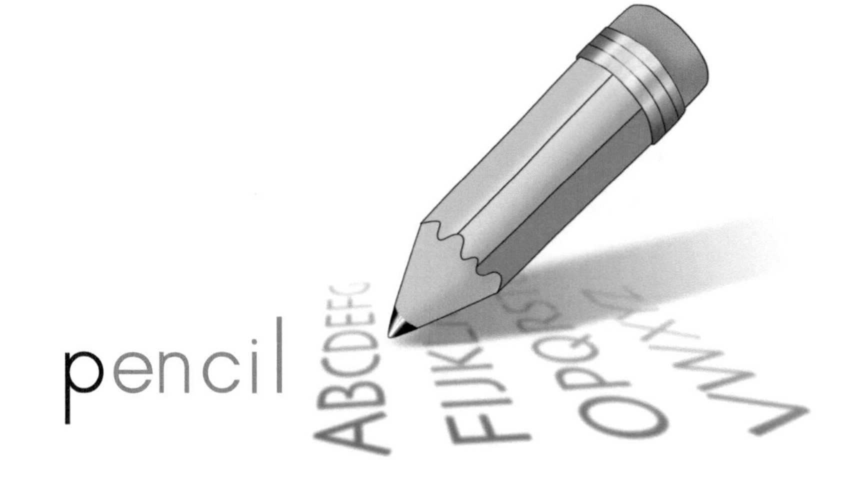

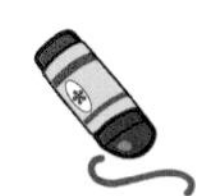

畫一畫
Trace the Lines

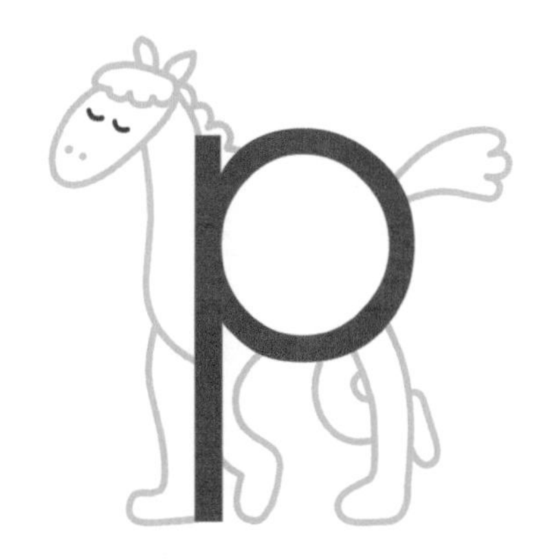
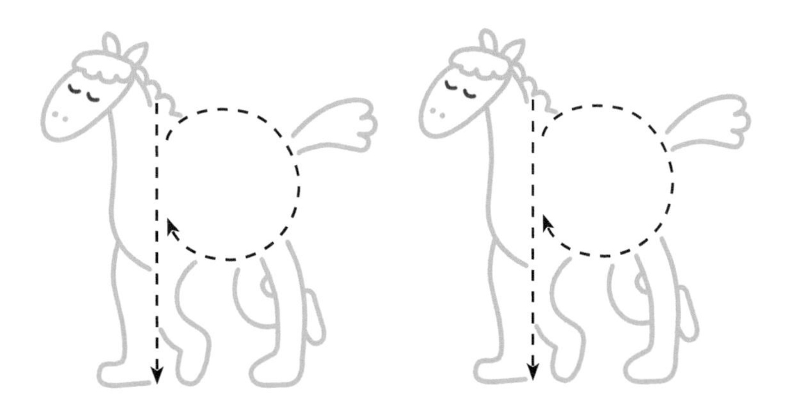

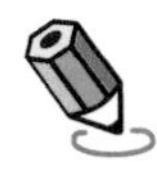

寫一寫
Trace and write

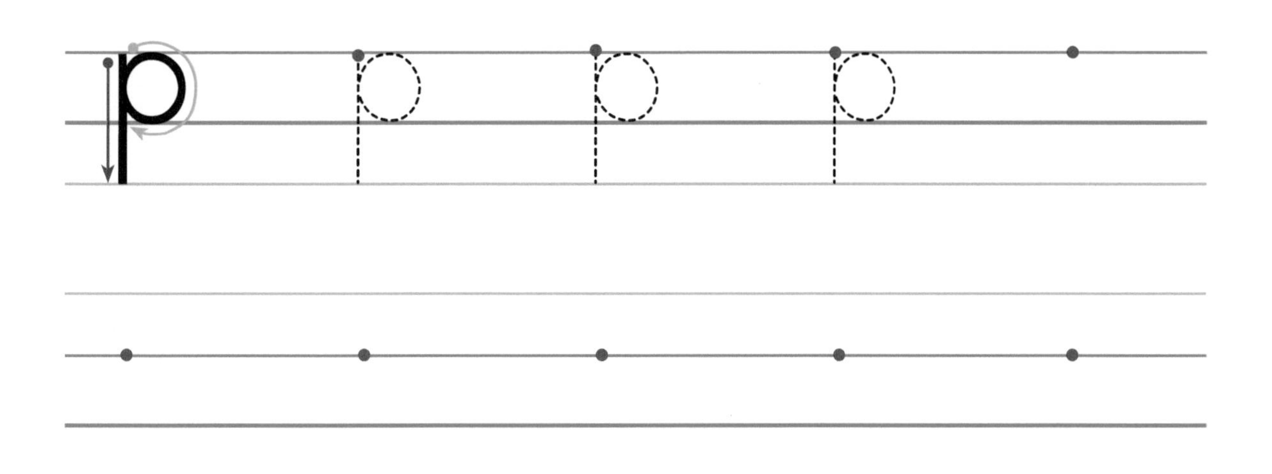

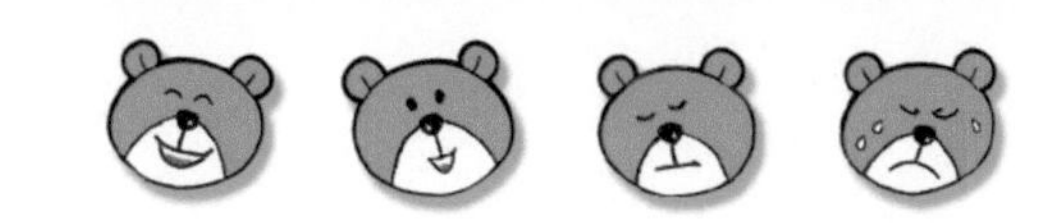

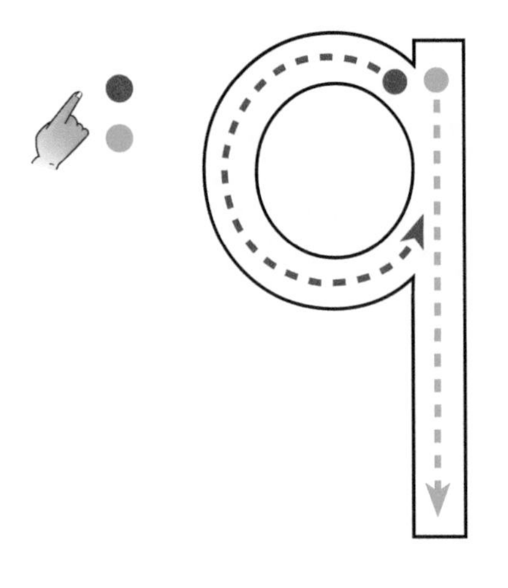

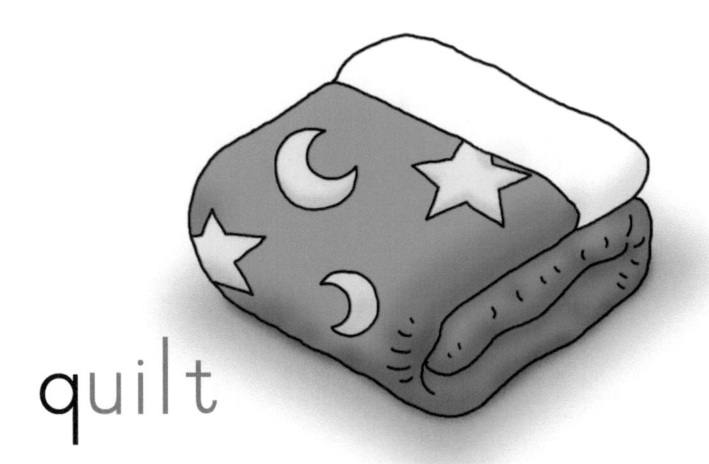

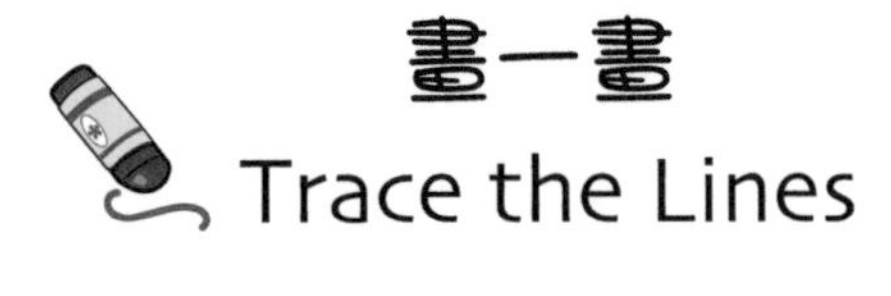

畫一畫
Trace the Lines

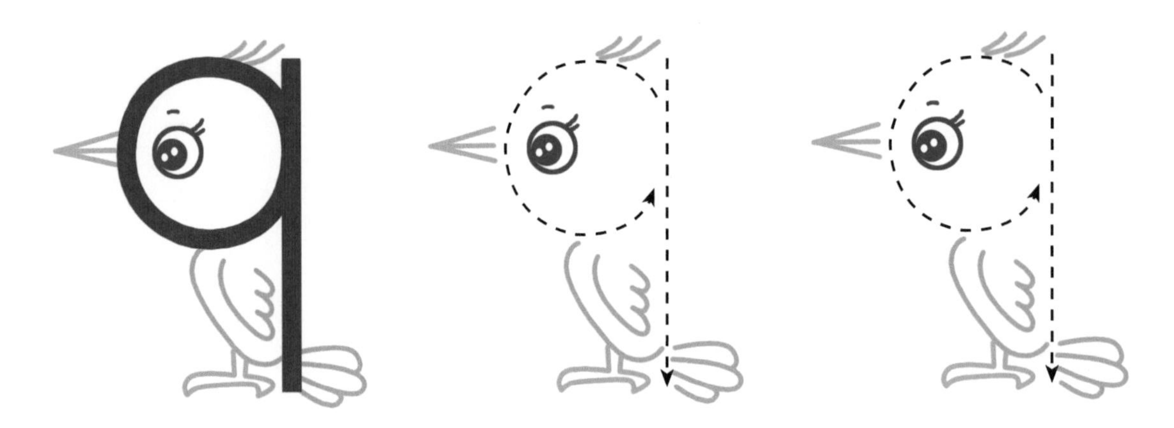

寫一寫
Trace and write

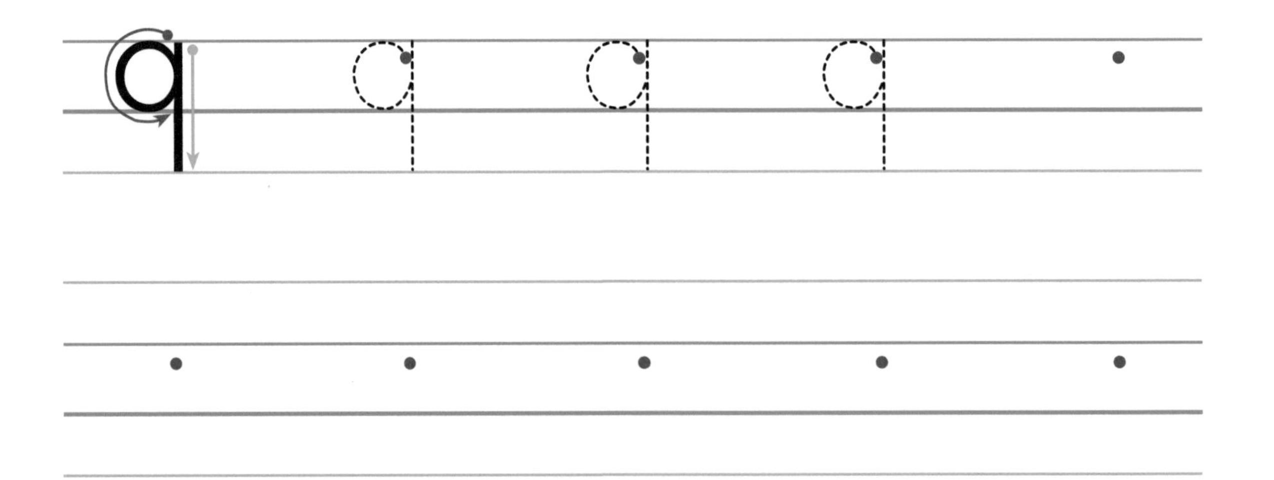

  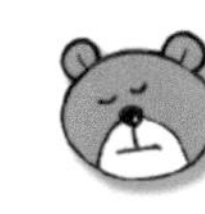 

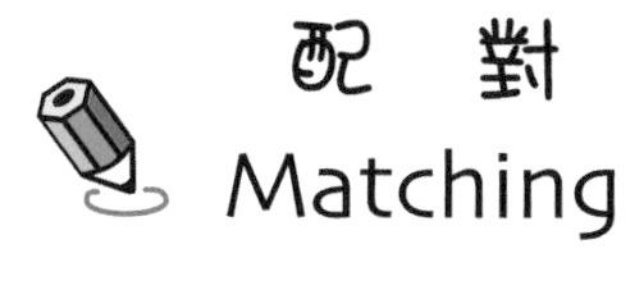

配對 Matching

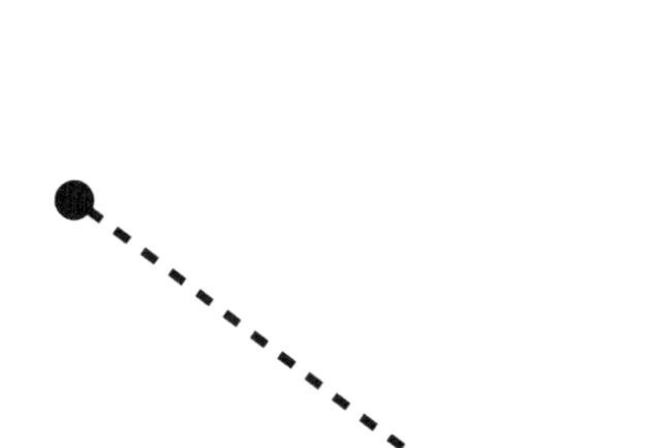

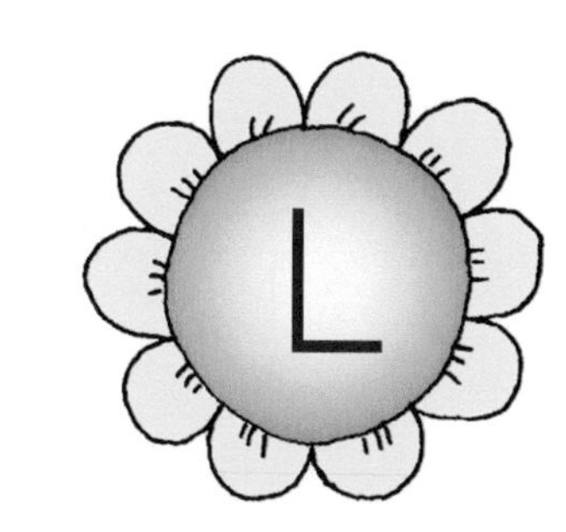

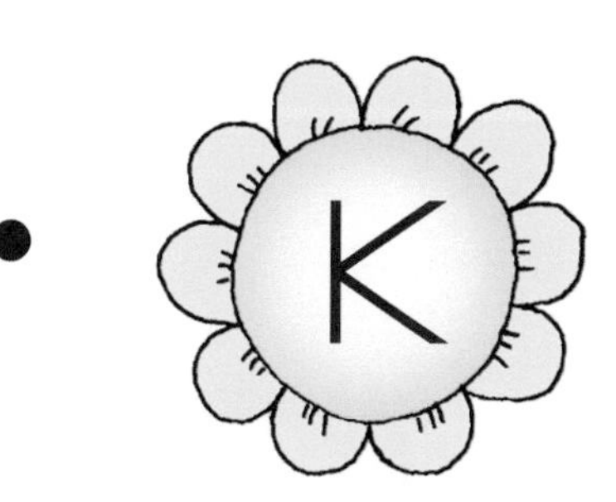

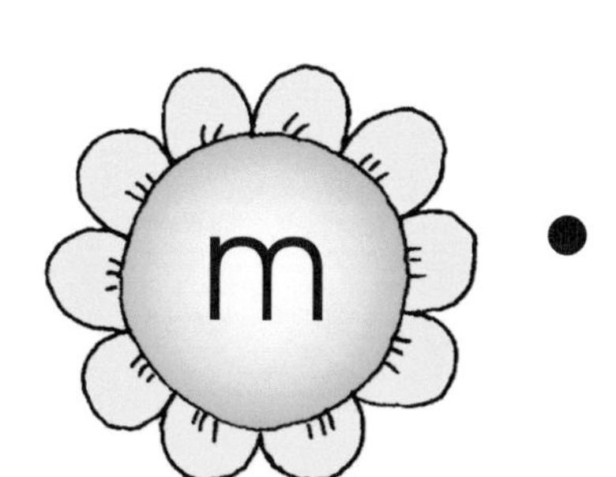

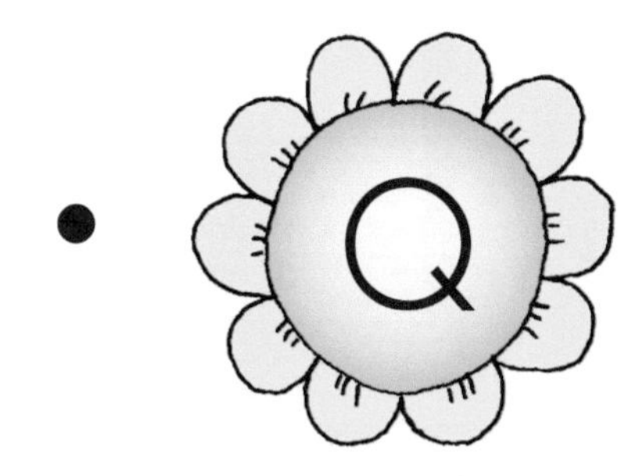

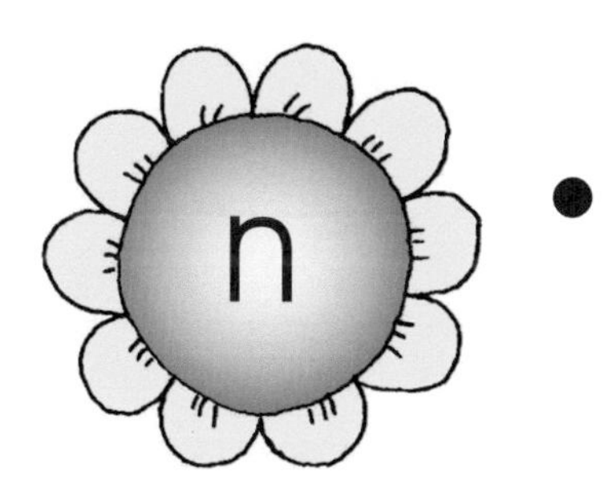

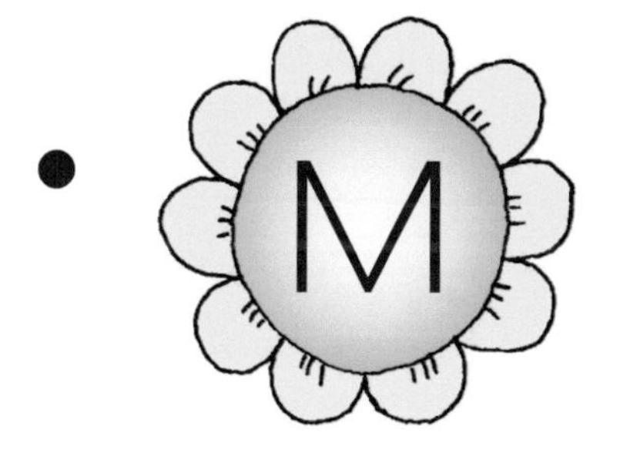

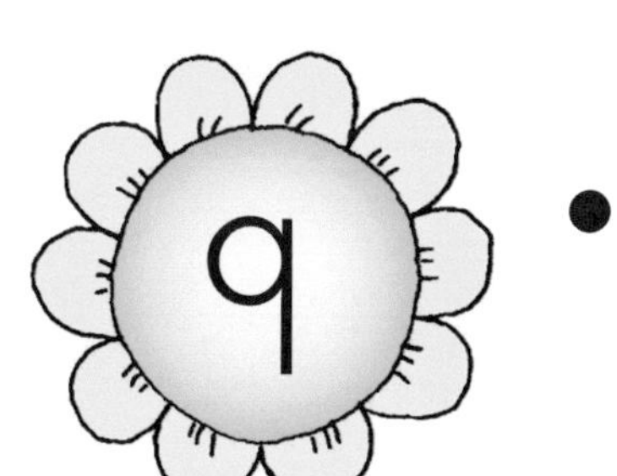

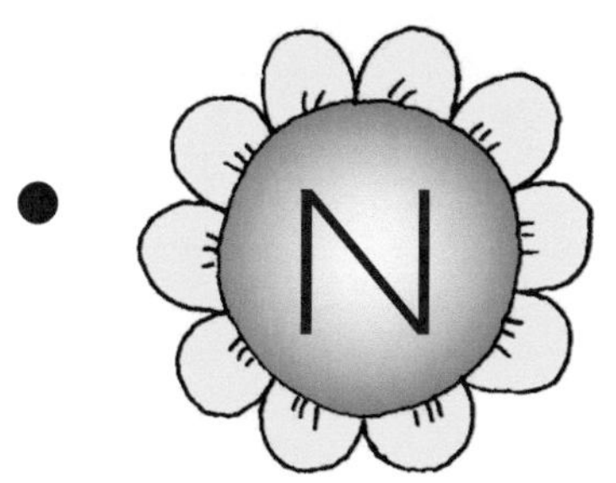

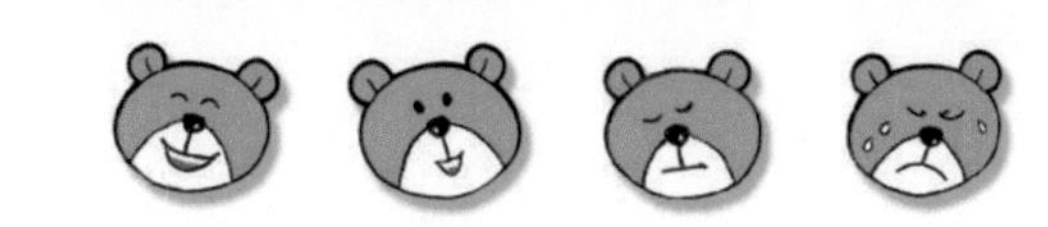

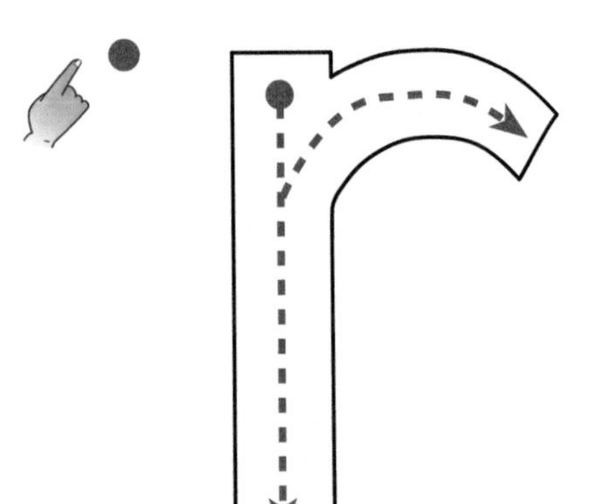

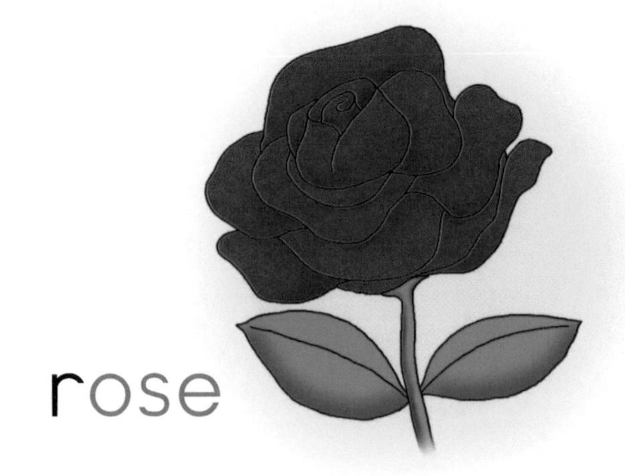

rose

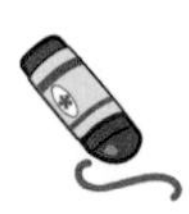

畫一畫
Trace the Lines

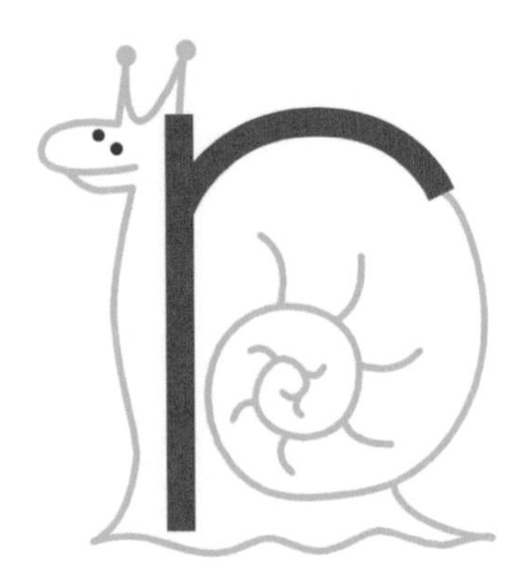

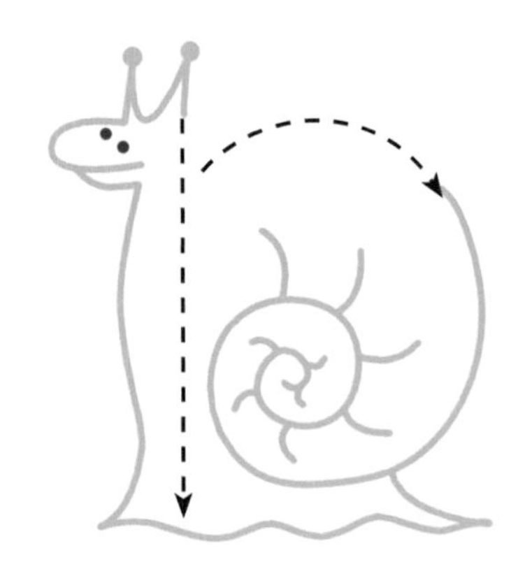

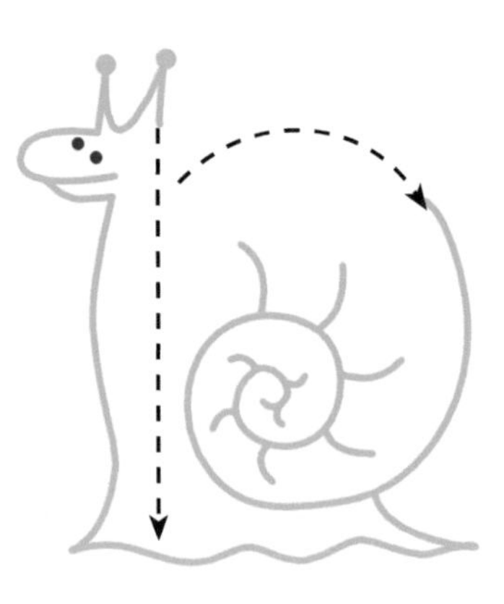

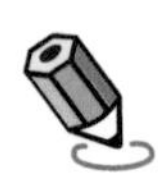

寫一寫
Trace and write

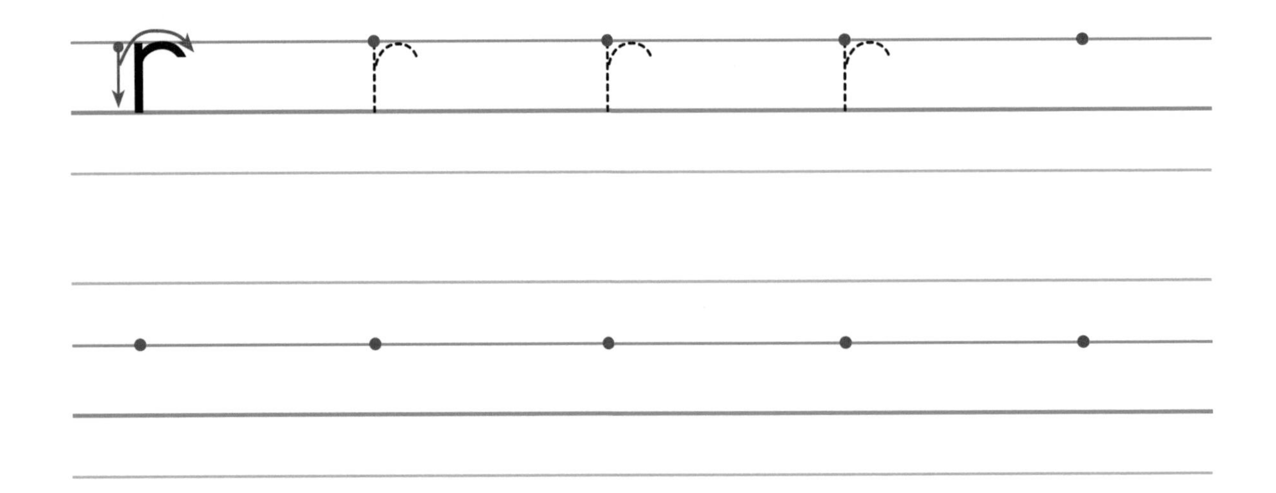

  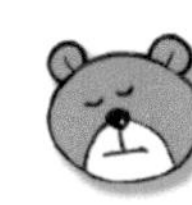 

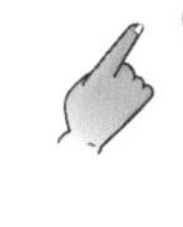
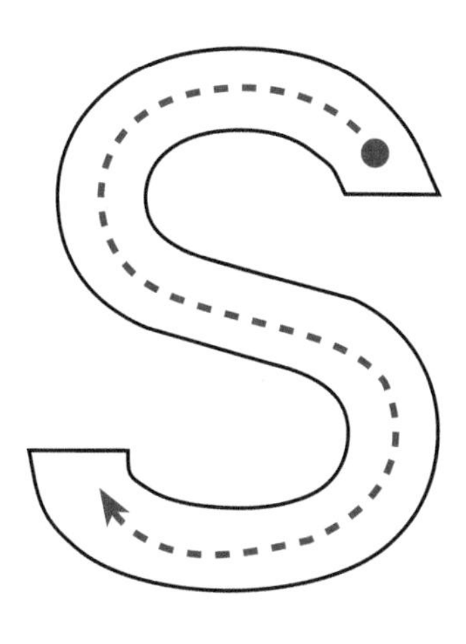

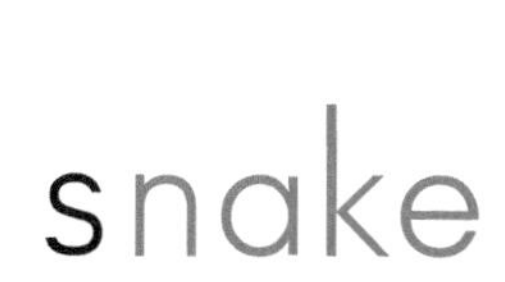
snake

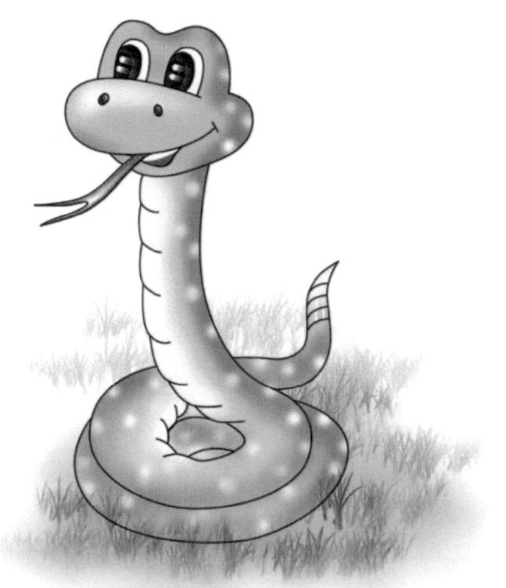

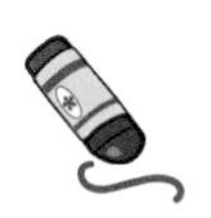
畫一畫
Trace the Lines

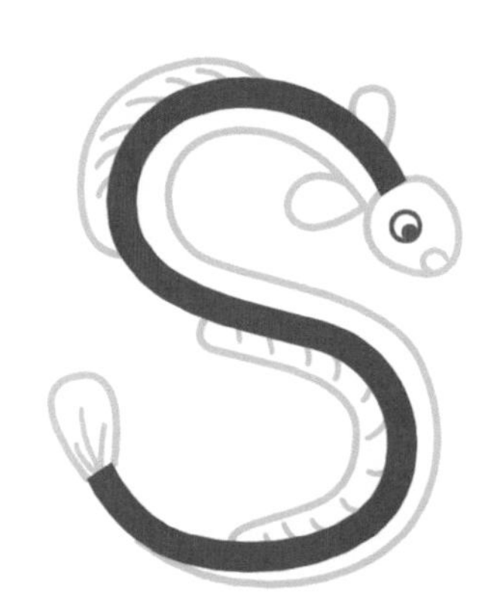 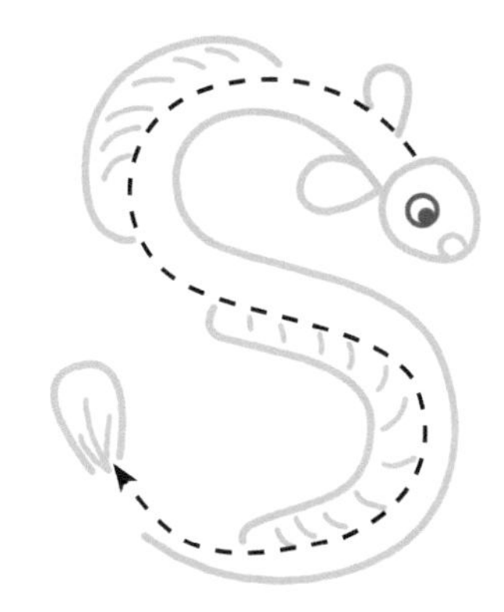 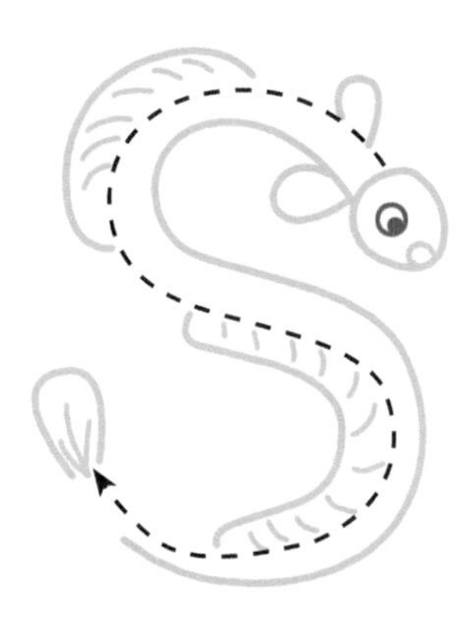

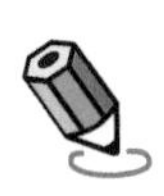
寫一寫
Trace and write

s s s s

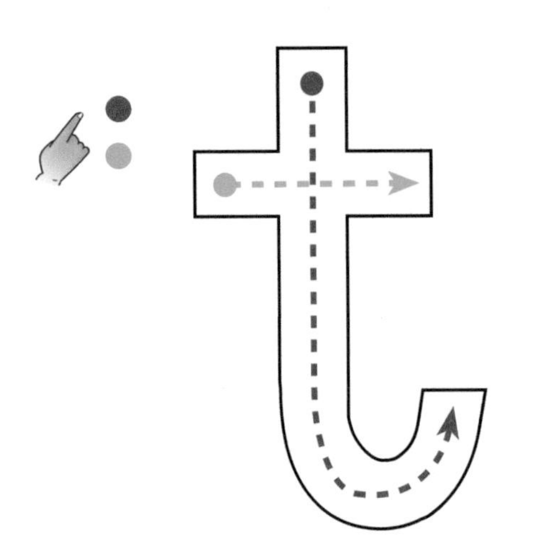

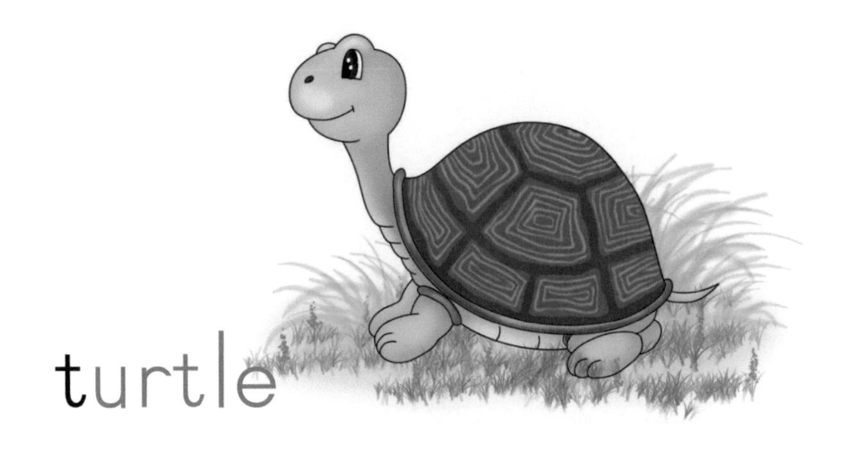

畫一畫
Trace the Lines

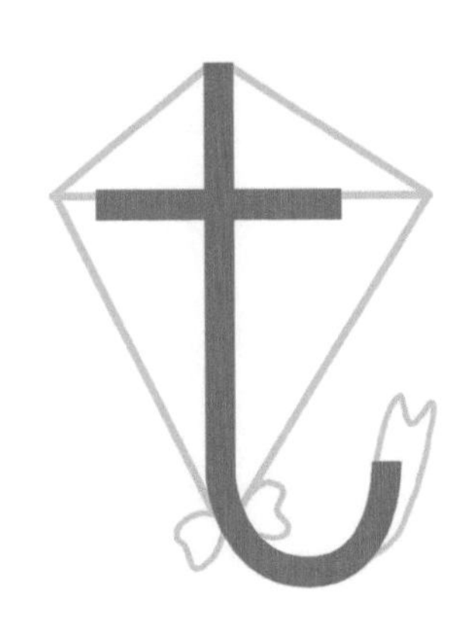

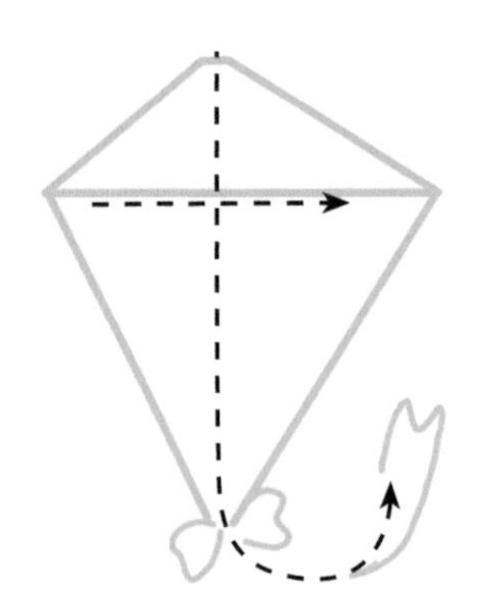

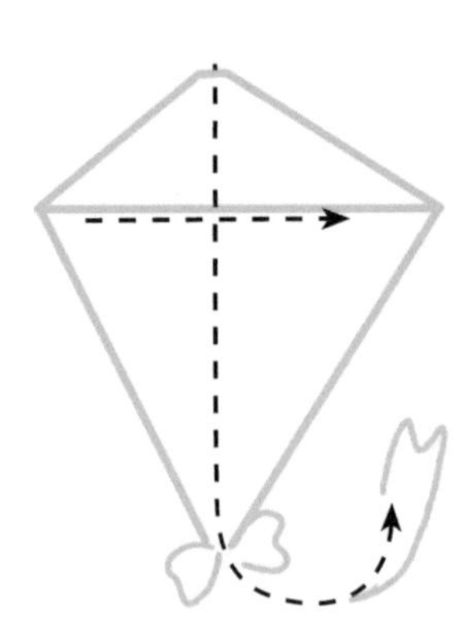

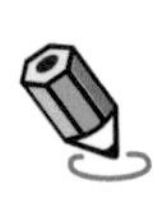

寫一寫
Trace and write

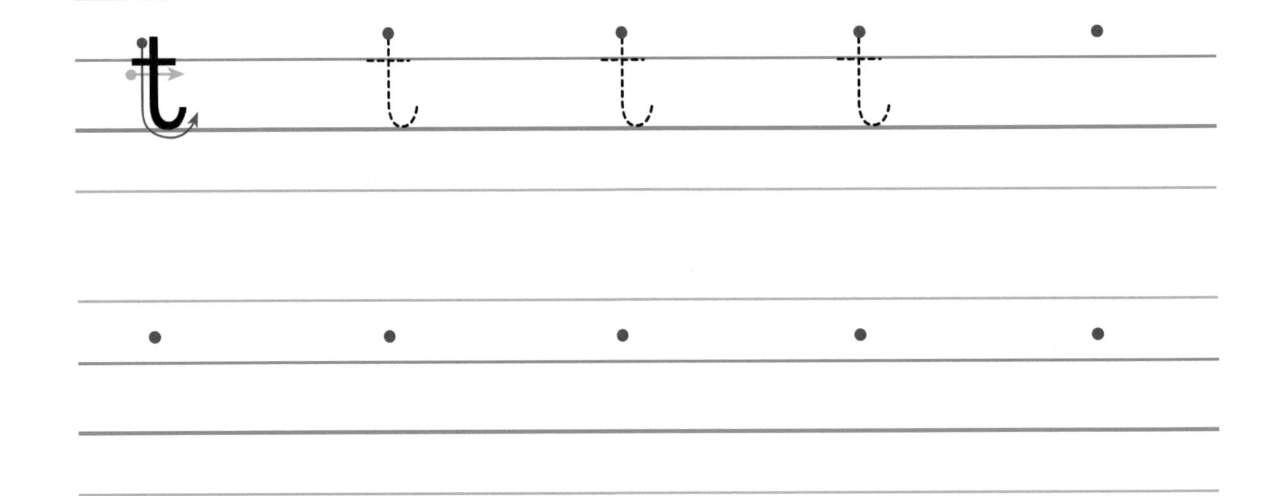

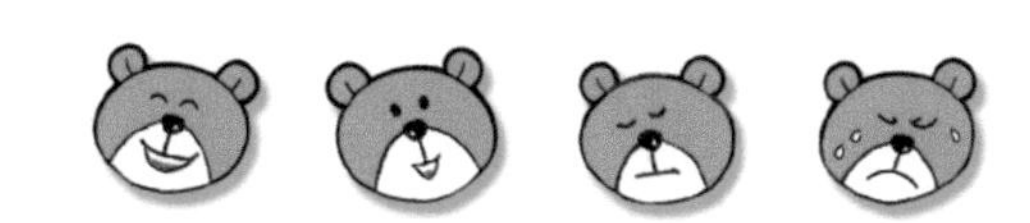

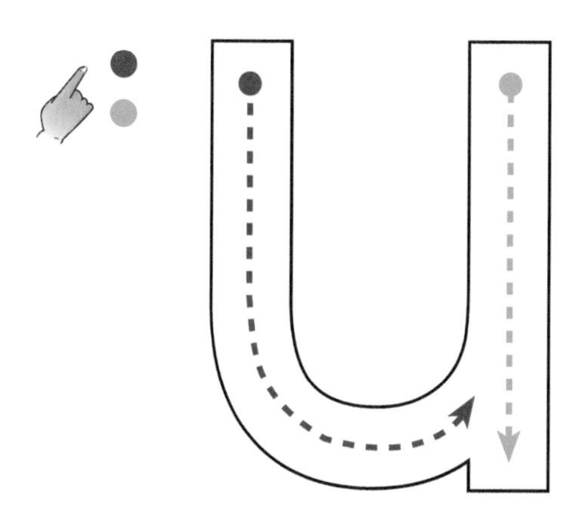

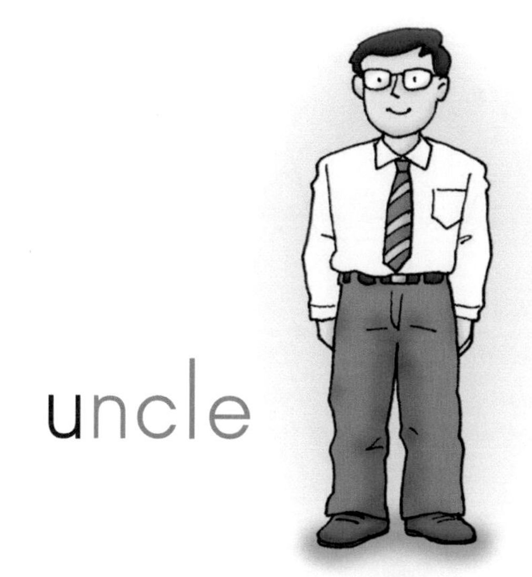
uncle

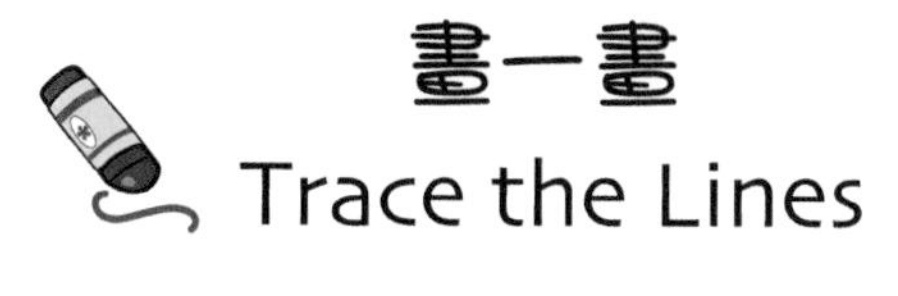
畫一畫
Trace the Lines

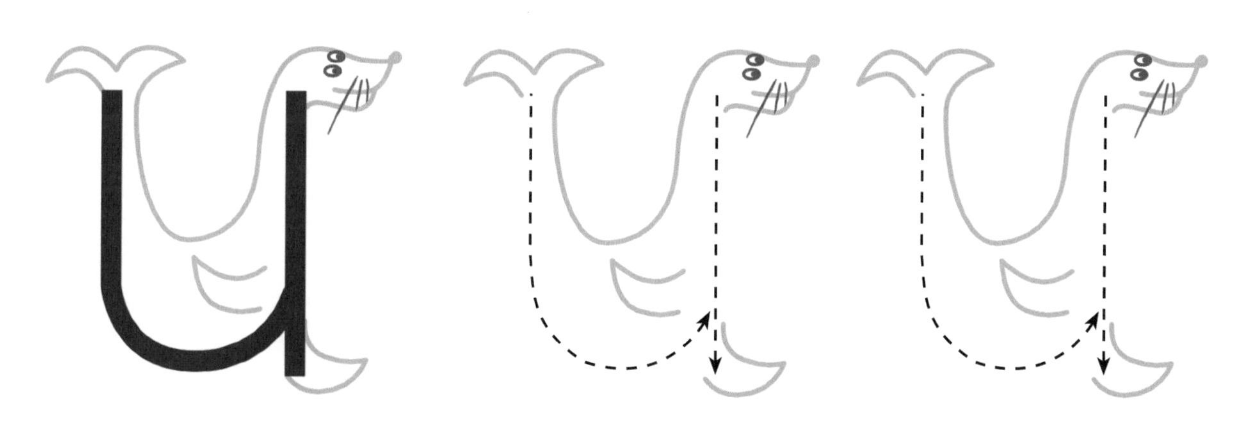

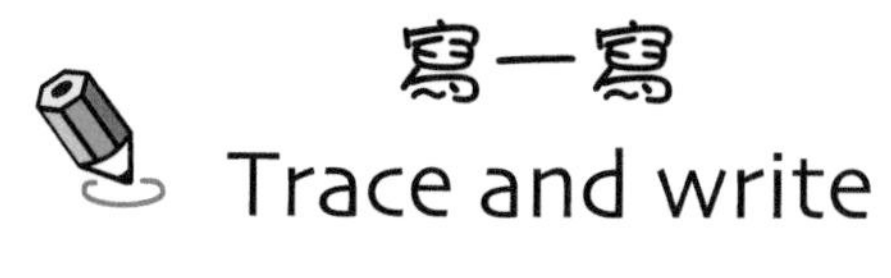
寫一寫
Trace and write

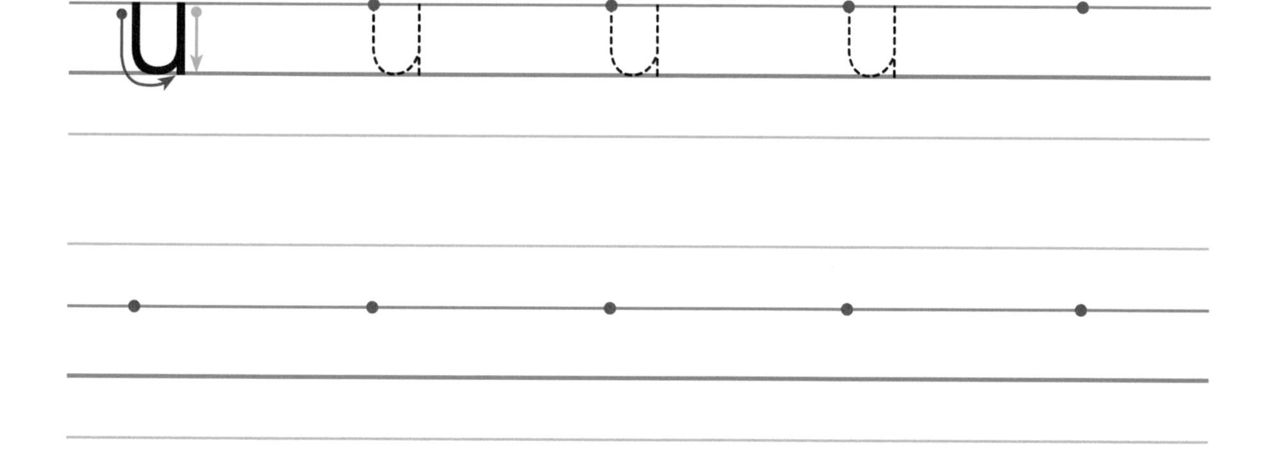

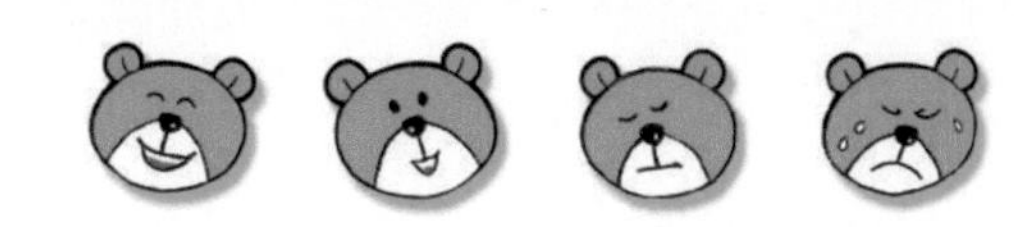

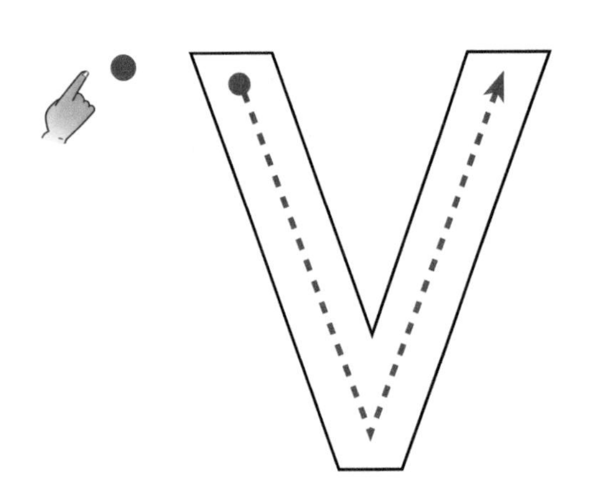

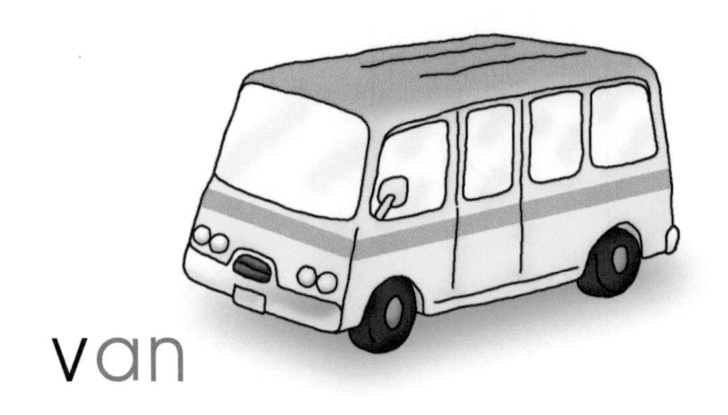

van

畫一畫
Trace the Lines

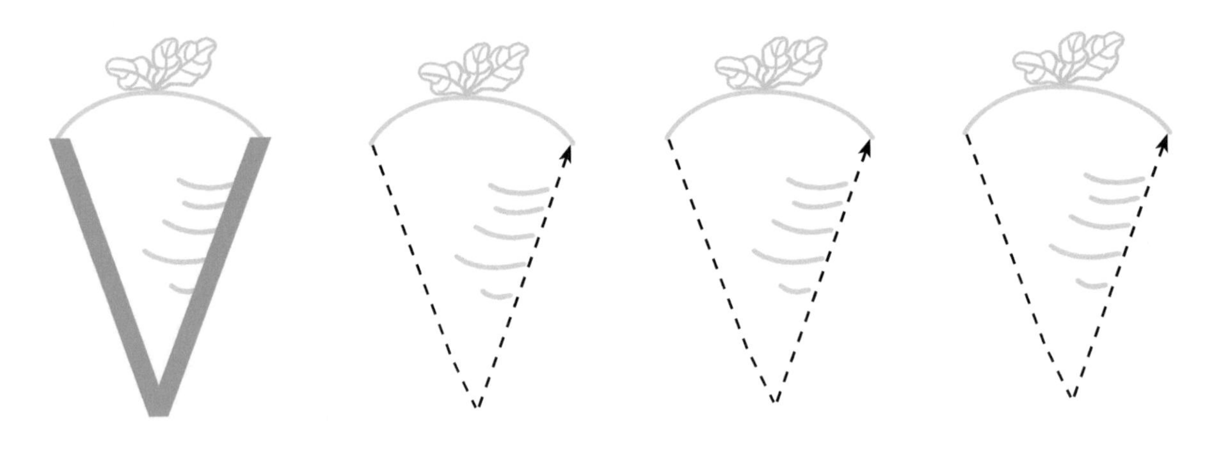

寫一寫
Trace and write

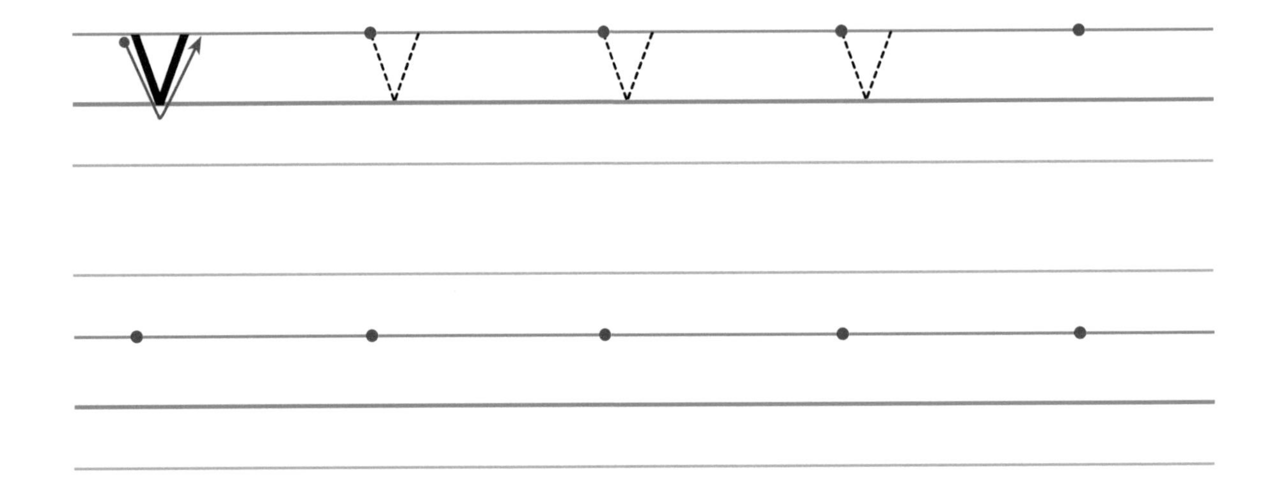

  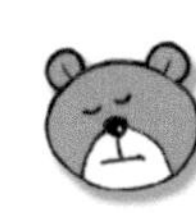 

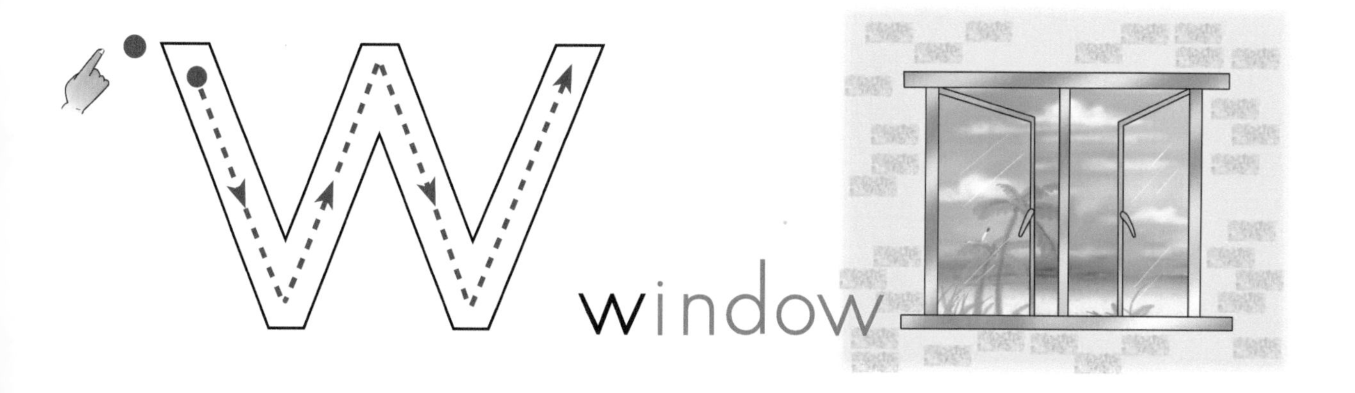

畫一畫
Trace the Lines

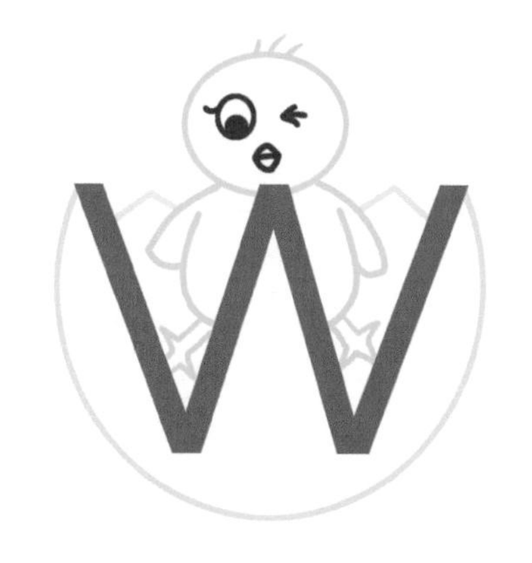

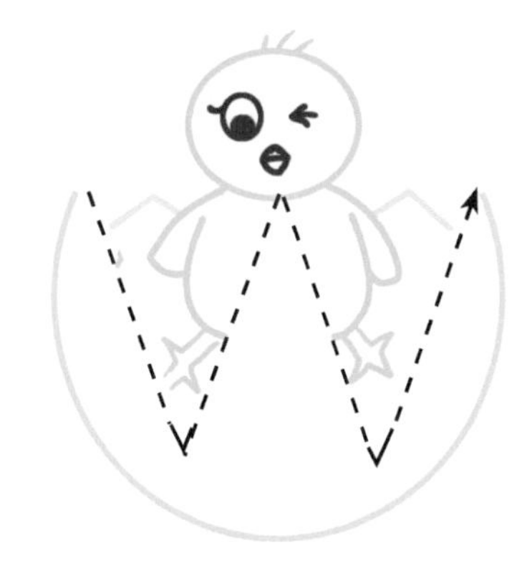
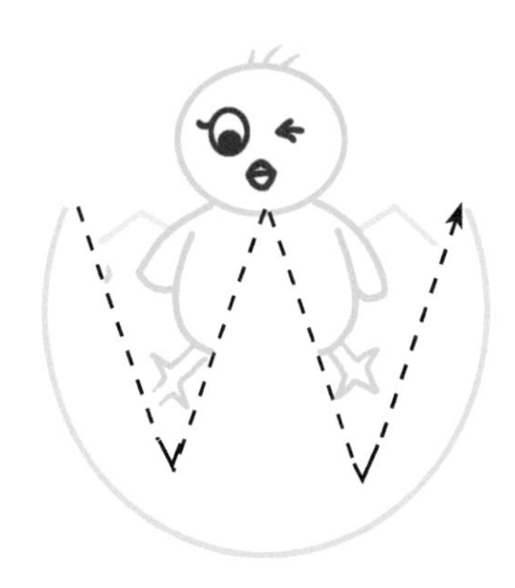

寫一寫
Trace and write

W

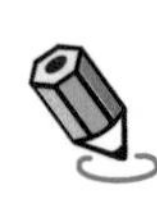

把字母國王身上的小楷字母填上顏色。

Please colour the small letters.

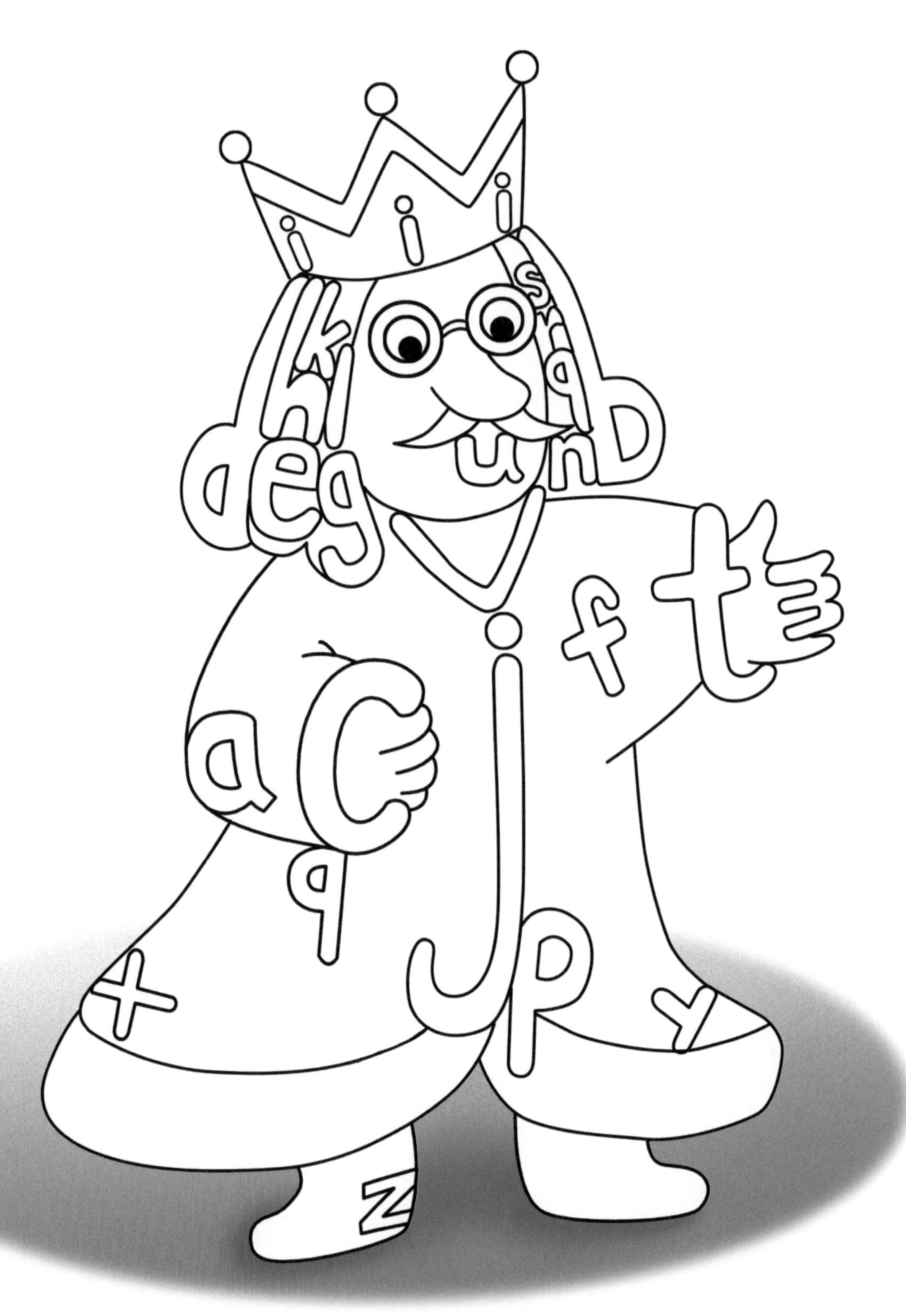

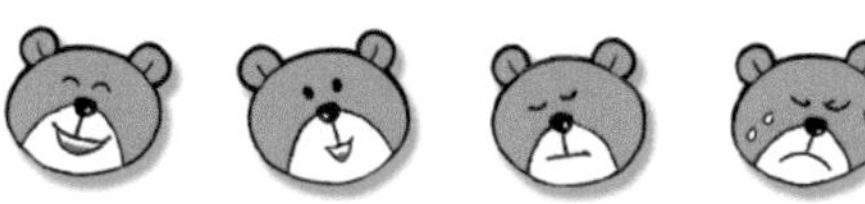
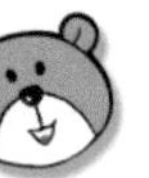
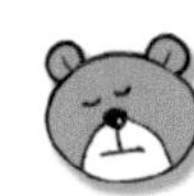

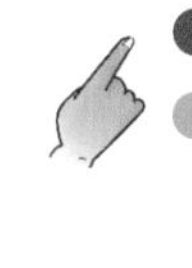
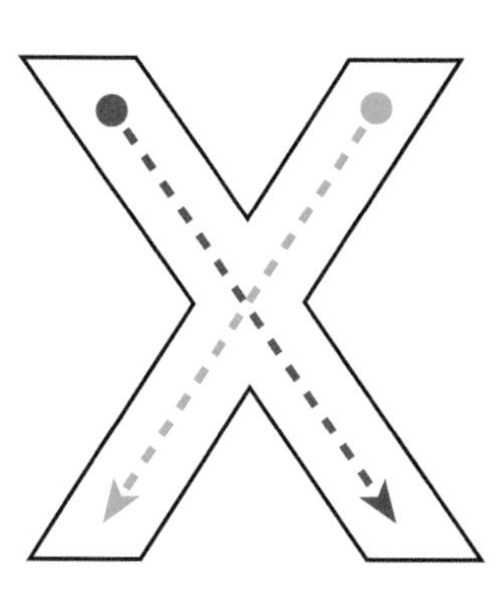

x-ray

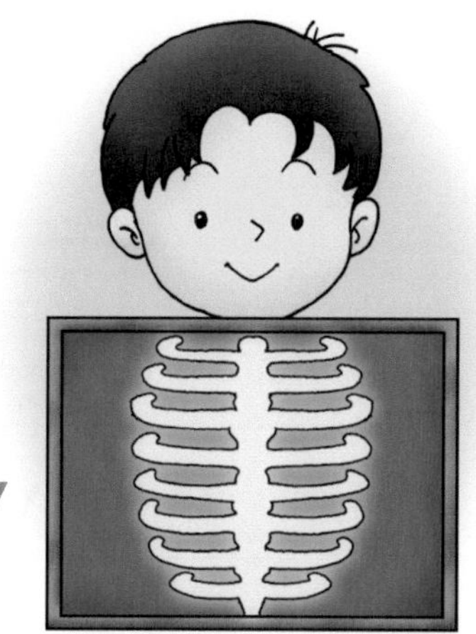

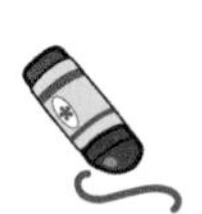
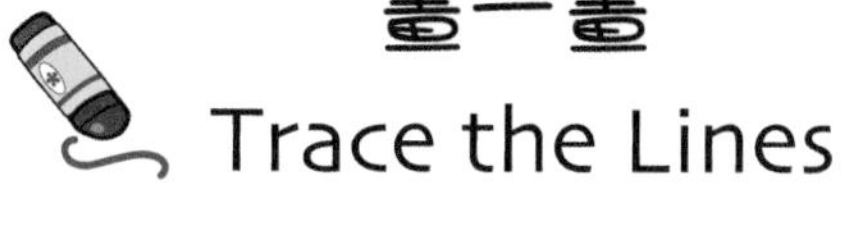

畫一畫

Trace the Lines

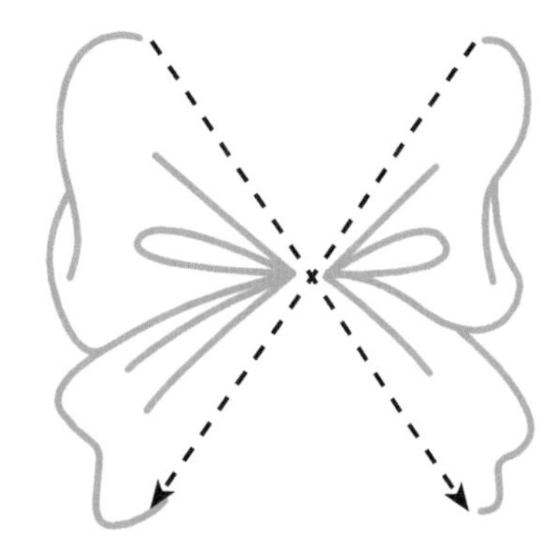
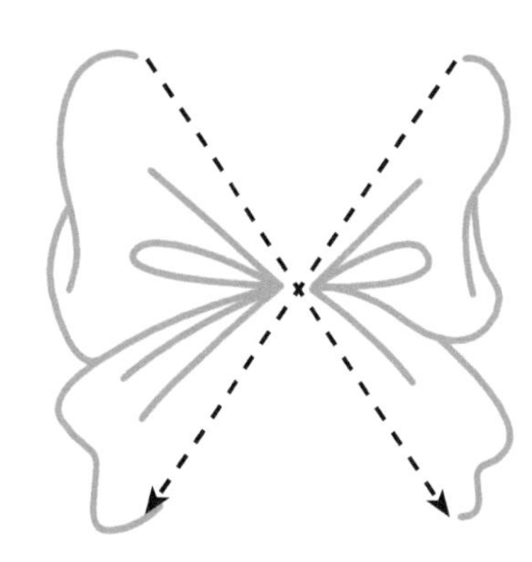

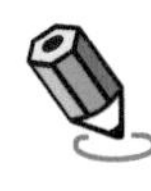

寫一寫

Trace and write

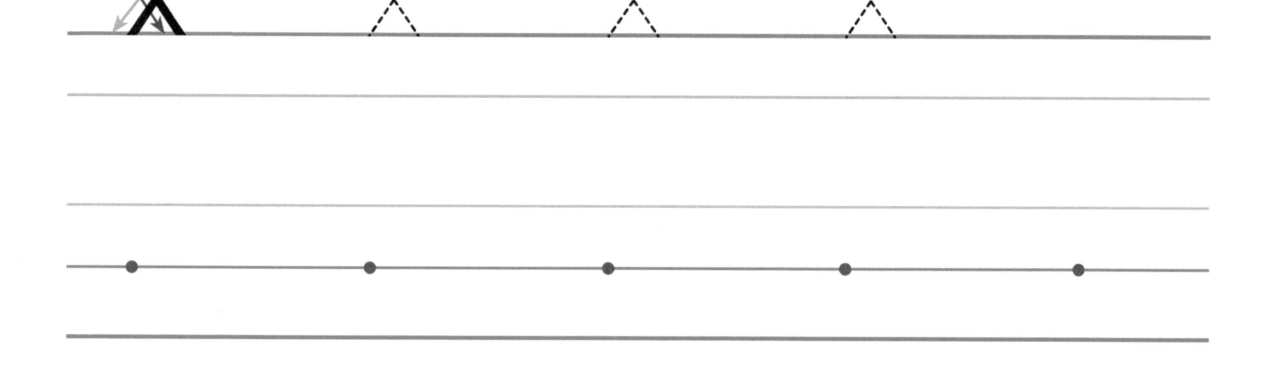

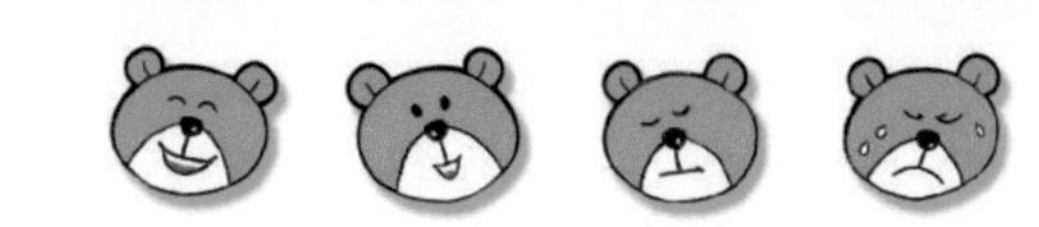

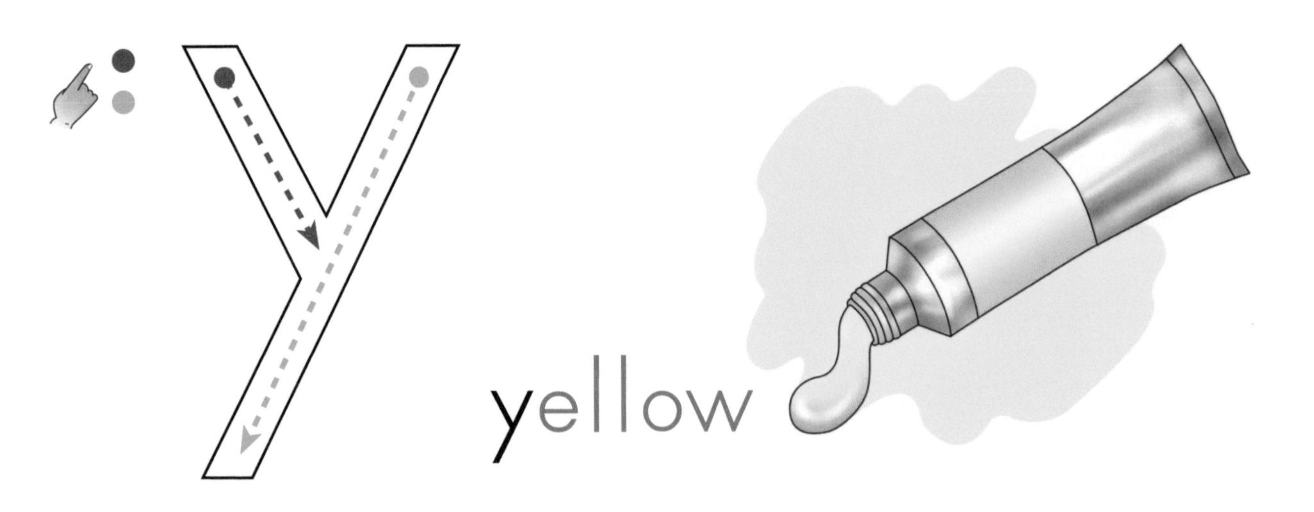

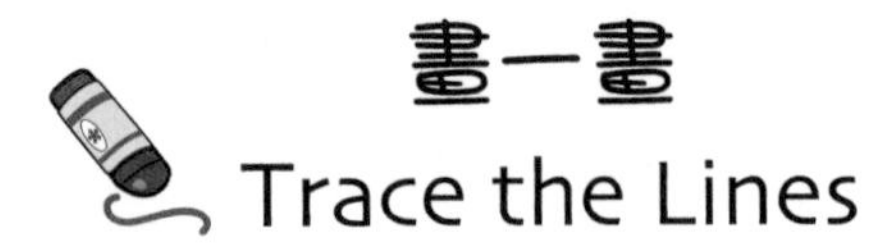

畫一畫
Trace the Lines

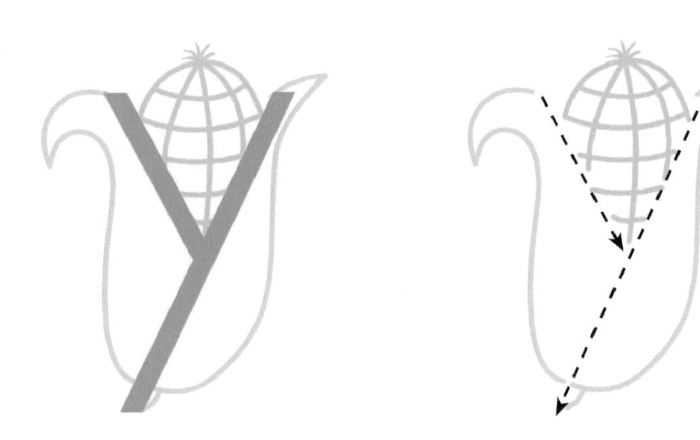

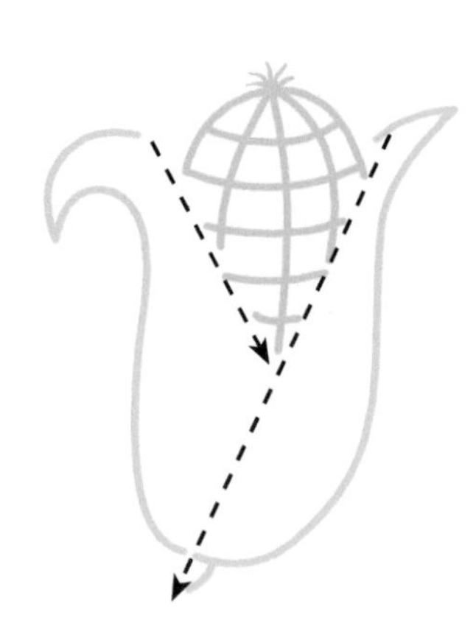

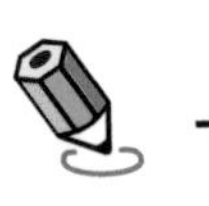

寫一寫
Trace and write

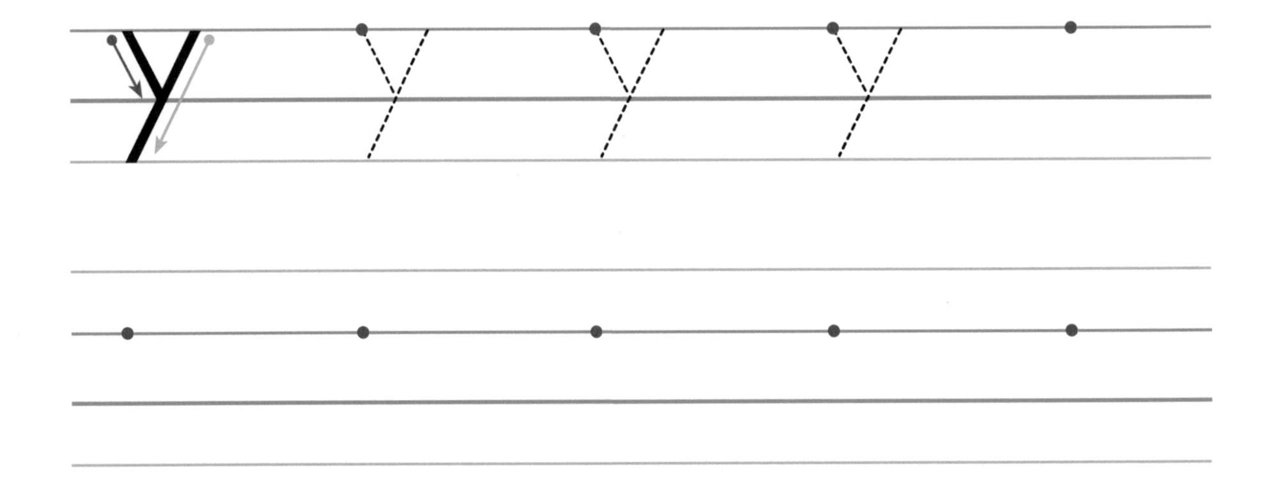

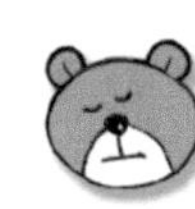

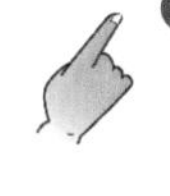
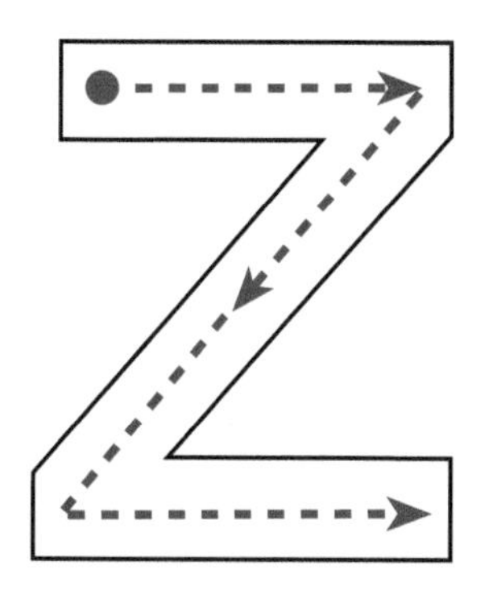
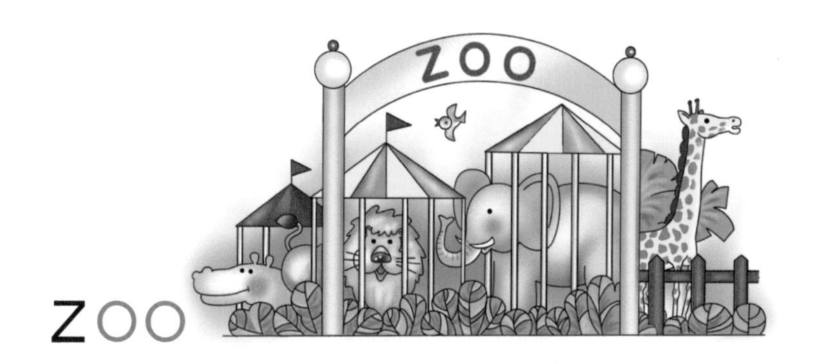

zoo

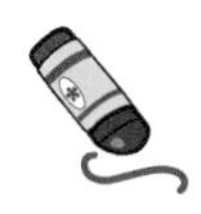

畫一畫

Trace the Lines

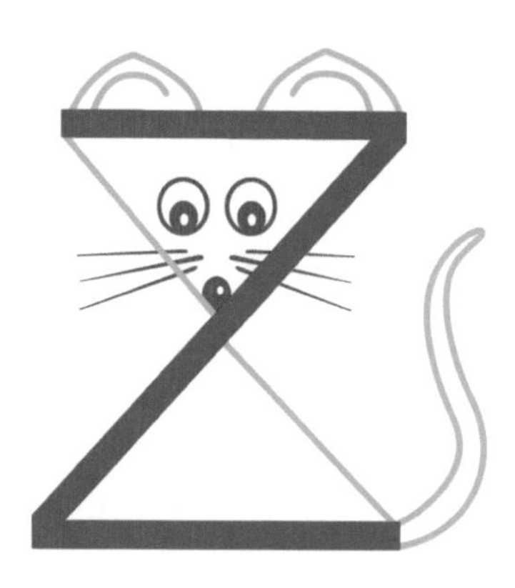
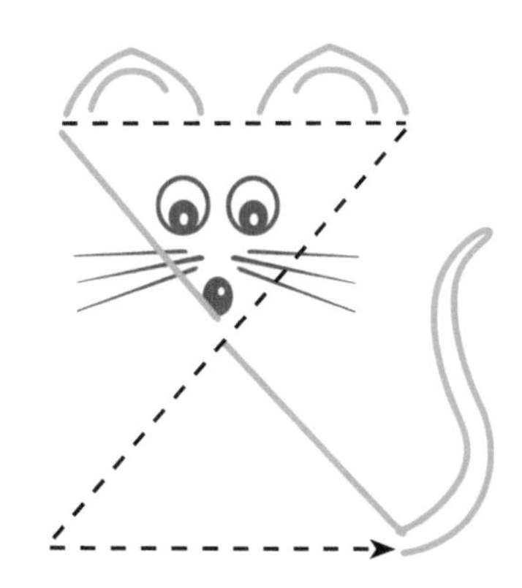
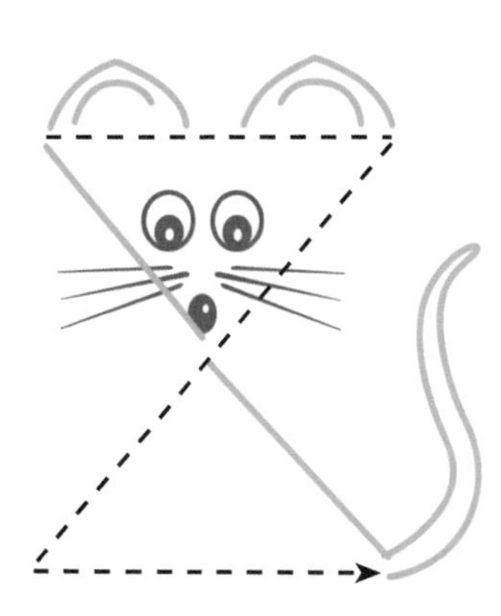

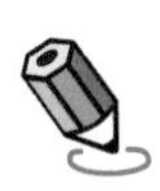

寫一寫

Trace and write

Z

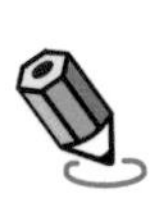

請順序把a～z連起來，然後把圖畫填上顏色。
Connect the dots from a~z. Colour the picture.

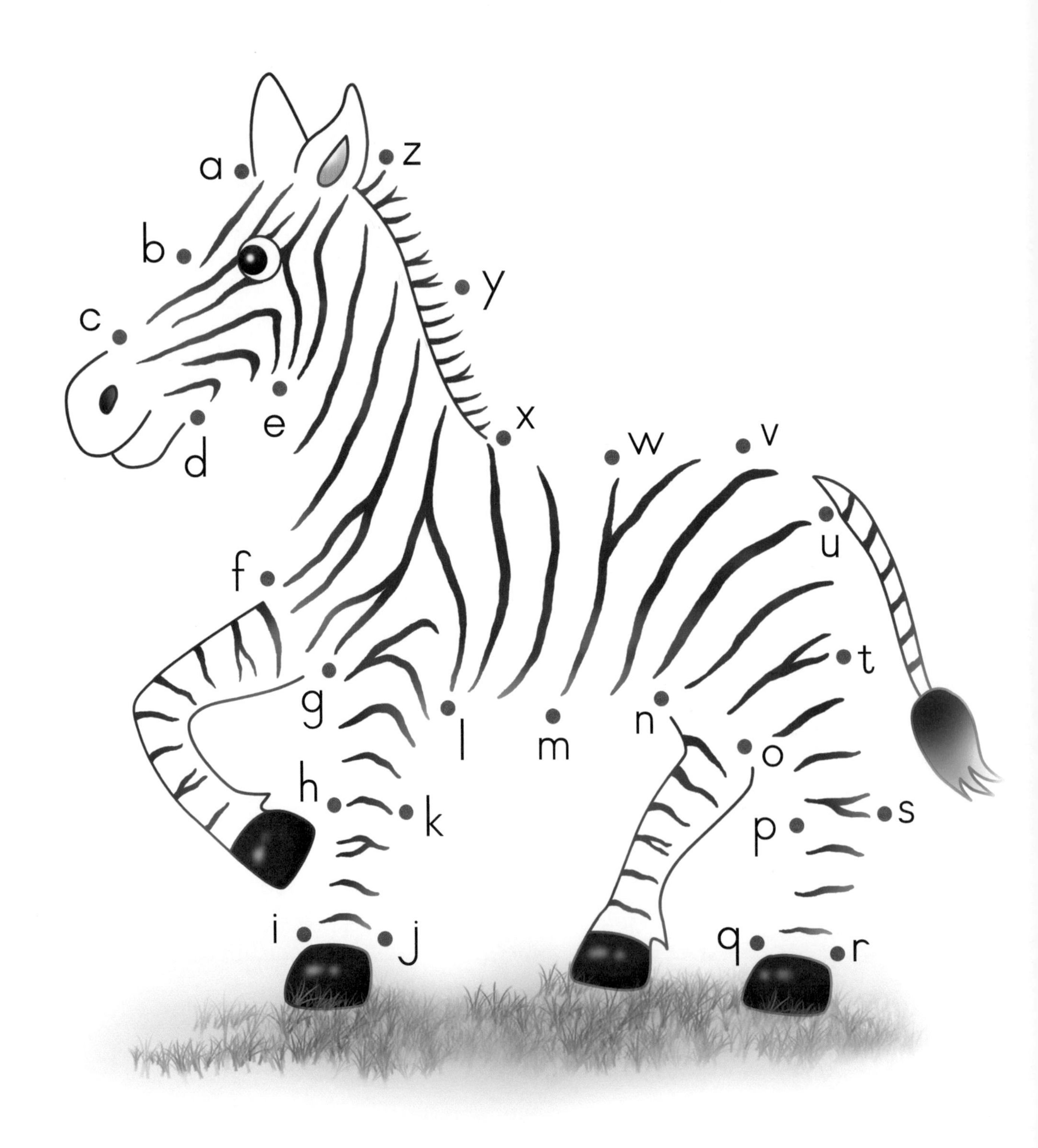

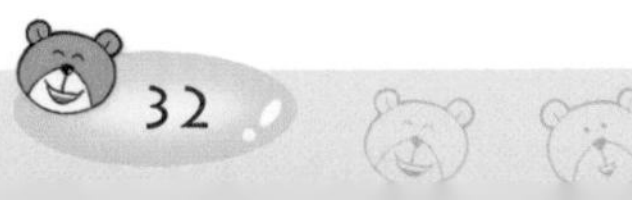